CONTEMPORARY RETAIL DESIGN

A STORE PLANNER'S HANDBOOK

Eddie Miles

CONTEMPORARY RETAIL DESIGN
A STORE PLANNER'S HANDBOOK

THE CROWOOD PRESS

First published in 2021 by
The Crowood Press Ltd
Ramsbury, Marlborough
Wiltshire SN8 2HR

enquiries@crowood.com
www.crowood.com

British Library Cataloguing-in-Publication Data
A catalogue record for this book is available from the British Library.

ISBN 978 1 78500 870 2

Front cover: Selfridges Women's Shoe Galleries, London. (Photo: Olivier Hess)

Frontispiece: Lush Liverpool

Cover design by Sergey Tsvetkov

Typeset by Simon and Sons
Printed and bound in India by Replika Press Pvt. Ltd.

Contents

The busy retail environment of Westfield World Trade Center, New York.

THE DESIRE TO TRADE, TO MAKE THINGS or to provide services for others to purchase sets human beings apart from the other species of our planet. The methods by which these trading transactions are carried out are bewildering in their variety and continue to evolve to meet the needs of the consumer. Retail today, meaning here the retailing of goods and services to the end-user rather than business-to-business wholesale trade, is something we encounter pretty much every day. We fill our baskets online just as we browse the shopping mall stores, sometimes still out of a need but also for reasons of entertainment, to pass the time or to counter boredom. The design of the many retail environments we encounter is as familiar to us as our home or workplace but this doesn't lessen the challenge faced by the retail designer when planning a new store. The design of a successful store will have answered a multitude of questions in its conception: does the store's planning allow it to function seamlessly? Are the materials used in the construction robust? Is the interior space a delight to visit? Does the design encourage shoppers to stay and spend their money? The intention of this book is to explain store design and construction so that the designer, student of design or retailer gains a thorough understanding of what it takes to make a great retail space. As an architect, I can tell you that the one certain thing a retail client will state with absolute conviction in their brief is the store opening date! To this end, the book also explains the practicalities of project planning from concept to store opening.

The effect of the coronavirus on the retail landscape of 2020 was of a scale unparalleled since the Second World War. For many retailers this was the final blow from which they could not recover, having already been affected by the rising costs of maintaining physical stores and the changing habits of customers. The retail world of today can therefore be a tough place, with shoppers' habits changing rapidly and in unforeseen ways. There seems no doubt that online retail will continue to take an increasing share of our spend, but I remain optimistic for the physical store and its unique place in our towns and cities. Whilst the pandemic has undoubtedly driven custom online, it seems it has also created an opportunity for local retailers who have built a customer base from the many people who no longer spend their working week away from home. Rapid change creates opportunity and there will be innovators emerging with new ideas that will draw us back to the mall, high street and department store. I hope that this book will offer practical guidance to the designers of such future stores that will cry out to be visited and where we will take delight in shopping.

TOBACCO

FOOD
DRINKS
TOBACCO

ANGUS

FRIBOURG
&
TREYER

Eighteenth-century storefront with
characteristic bow-fronted oriel
windows in London's Haymarket.

Chapter One

Store Types and Their History

ORIGIN OF THE STORE

Market Trading

The typical high street store can trace its lineage back to the markets of the Middle Ages. The market served as a meeting place to allow producers of goods, primarily foodstuffs, to barter or sell their products. Equally, the market was where imported goods were sold by merchants who had played no part in their actual production. As trading practices were codified and regulated, so the rights of towns to hold markets were controlled through charters which sought to control which goods could be sold and by whom. By the thirteenth century, the market square was established and remains a feature today in many European towns and cities. The relationship between market buyer and market seller seems to have been an unequal one. Without the systems of distribution we know today, the effects of scarcity and local shortages would have been acutely felt by buyers and much of the control over market trade was intended to protect the consumer from sharp practice. As well as the open-air marketplace, the stalls could be organized to trade from a market hall under the control of the municipality who oversaw trading practices, rules and regulations such as the control of weights and measures. As the markets developed, so did the traders' temporary stalls which were designed to display and to protect merchandise. These stalls became semi-permanent and by the fourteenth century examples of permanent structures are found, some of two storeys with the owners' living quarters on the floor above.

John Stow's *Survey of London*, published in 1598, describes this development in his recollection of how Old Fish Street in the City of London had developed in his time:

> ... these houses, now possessed by fishmongers, were at the first but moveable boards (or stalls), set out on market-days, to show their fish there to be sold; but procuring license to set up sheds, they grew to shops, and by little and little to tall houses, of three or four stories in height, and now are called Fish street.

By the early part of the seventeenth century, a new consumer society was emerging in London. By the mid 1600s, London's population stood at over half a million, a five-fold increase over a hundred years. The growth in population also concentrated the wealthy in a single city which began to draw in products and consumer goods from the provinces and further afield. London thus became the focus of politics, culture and consumerism, populated and visited by gentry and nobility with the means to spend ostentatiously. Contemporary records, such as the diaries of Samuel Pepys and John Evelyn, give today's reader a fascinating insight into the retail world of the mid 1600s. Here, for instance, is John Evelyn's account of his visit to Paris on 3 February 1664: 'Here is a shop called NOAH'S ARK, where are sold all curiosities, natural or artificial, Indian or European, for luxury or use, as cabinets, shells, ivory, porcelain, dried fishes, insects, birds, pictures, and a thousand exotic extravagances.'

Evelyn's contemporary Samuel Pepys includes in his diary (1660–69) frequent references to the London shops he visits. These include a glove and ribbon shop, drapers, goldsmiths, bookshops, victuallers, a cane shop, a periwig shop and a watchmaker. Clearly, by the Restoration, the major European cities could boast an array of shops selling a wide variety of luxury goods to wealthy consumers.

On 22 September 1666, and in the aftermath of the Great Fire of London of that year, we find Pepys bemoaning the lack of availability of glaziers: 'My glazier, indeed, is so full of worke that I cannot get him to come to perfect my house'. The window glass of this time was not the flat, clear material we know today, but rather an imperfect, greenish-tinted sheet that was made from blown glass, cut into a cylinder and then re-heated and flattened. This glass, known as broad window glass, produced only limited-sized glass sheets. Another technique was that of crown glass manufacture, where a bubble of molten glass was spun to form a circular sheet, leaving a 'crown' of thicker glass in the middle. In the 1660s in France, Lucas De Néhou improved the size of glass sheets through the rolling of glass on an iron table and this technique was perfected over the next century so that by 1800, glass production in Europe was industrialized, making larger, more consistent glass sheets cheaper and more widely available. The size and quality of glass in the eighteenth century no doubt influenced the storefront which typically comprised bow-fronted oriel windows on either side of the main entrance door. The bow windows were typically the only source of natural light, with the lighting supplemented with oil lamps. This no doubt limited the depth of the store, with the rear portion being given over to a 'back shop', divided from the 'fore shop' by a decorative screen. As of now, retailers occasionally went to great expense to fit out their stores, as we learn from contemporary accounts.

Daniel Defoe's 1726 work *The Complete English Tradesman* was intended, in the author's words, as 'a collection of useful instructions for a young tradesman' and he defined tradesmen as 'all other shopkeepers, who do not actually work upon, make, or manufacture, the goods they sell'. Defoe offers us a fascinating insight into the business of setting up a store in London in the eighteenth century, starting by selecting the right location:

> For a tradesman to open his shop in a place unresorted to, or in a place where his trade is not agreeable, and where it is not expected, it is no wonder if he has no trade. What retail trade would a milliner have among the fishmongers' shops on Fishstreet-hill, or a toyman about Queen-hithe?

Whilst acknowledging that an attractive store attracts new customer, Defoe warns those establishing a new retail store of excessive expenditure when coming to fit out their premises. He describes the retail interior of his day as painted and gilded, with decorative wall tiles and fitted out with fine shelves, glass-fronted display cases, mirrors, wall sconces and lanterns. From his account we understand the interior to be of high quality, in the classical style and well adorned

Stores or Shops?

Like any commercial sector or specialist interest group, the retail business has its own lexicon, and this can lead to confusion and misunderstanding. Most shoppers in the UK would no doubt describe their destination on a shopping trip as a 'shop'. Amongst those who take a professional interest in retail, these shoppers are headed for a 'store'. The use of the word 'store' to describe the selling space (both physical and online) has its origins in the US, but it is now so widely used across the industry as to render the noun 'shop' redundant. This book will therefore follow the convention of using the word 'store' and its derivatives: store design, store planning and so on.

The word 'shop' exists as a verb, as in 'it's fun to shop at a new store'. Further possible confusion can arise if we consider the word 'store' in its original meaning, meaning a place where things are stored. In the retail world, the storeroom is designated the 'stockroom'.

with displays to show merchandise to best advantage. This certainly appears to have been common for high-end retail in the eighteenth century; little evidence exists to confirm how far down the market such techniques were used. I shall leave the final word to Defoe, who expresses his contempt for those spending extravagantly on shop fit-out: 'So that, in short, here was a trade which might be carried on for about £30 or £40 stock, required £300 expenses to fit up the shop, and make a show to invite customers.'

Emergence of the Modern Store

By the nineteenth century, retail was booming, with many more stores opening and existing stores embracing changes in fashion. Charles Dickens, writing in the 1830s, observed this modernization of the store in one of his *Sketches by Boz*:

> Quiet, dusty old shops in different parts of town, were pulled down; spacious premises with stuccoed fronts and gold letters, were erected instead; floors were covered with Turkey carpets; roofs supported by massive pillars; doors knocked into windows; a dozen squares of glass into one; one shopman into a dozen …

The Glass Excise Act was abolished in 1845, ending a century of a tax originally introduced to raise money to fund Britain's wars in the American colonies. The affordability of glass, both through the easing of taxation and the industrialization of its manufacture, allowed engineers and architects to create new forms not hitherto seen: the best-known example of this was Joseph Paxton's Crystal Palace, created for the Great Exhibition of 1851. Paxton's structures relied on a framework of precast iron elements. Likewise, cast and wrought iron was indeed making its mark on the design of industrial and retail buildings, allowing for greater spans between walls and more open storefronts. Thus, by the mid-1800s we see the emergence of retail spaces that are even more recognizable as the stores we know in our own age. Other technologies that contributed to this were the widespread adoption of gas lighting in the 1820s and electric lighting from the end of the same century. By way of illustration as to how fast the modern retail store developed from this point, it was in 1909 that Harry Gordon Selfridge opened the first phase of what was to become Selfridges on London's Oxford Street. His department store was purpose-built and fitted with electric lighting, lifts, a sprinkler system and large glazed display windows and entrance doors.

The early part of the twentieth century saw a growing middle class with the means to spend a greater part of their income on consumer goods and services than ever before. This led to an increase in the number of stores, and to their concentration in our

Asprey's late nineteenth-century cast iron and plate glass storefront in London's New Bond Street.

high streets. With greater choice available to the consumer, Edwardian-era customer service became a vital part of retailing, reflected in Selfridge's maxim 'The customer is always right'. The early 1900s also saw the advent of the nationwide chain store, with the founding of Nordstrom, Walgreens, J.C. Penney, Neiman Marcus and Woolworth's in the US. In Germany, the two department store groups Peek & Cloppenburg and KaDeWe were founded; the UK saw the start of Burton's, Dorothy Perkins and Waitrose. It could be argued that retailers' desire to have a presence in every major town or city in their home country, and in the latter decades of the twentieth century to establish a global presence, has resulted in a bland uniformity in our shopping experience. The counter-position is that the consumer now enjoys access to a global market, undreamt of in earlier eras. The establishment of nationwide and global retail brands has demanded not only a consistency of merchandise, service and price but also a standard of retail design to be applied across a brand's estate. Store design must not only function as a space to display and sell but equally must explain the brand, tell the story of the brand and promote the values of the brand.

STORE TYPES

Before we start to dissect the store and explore store design, it is worth taking a brief survey of the distinct types of retail space that exist.

High Street Stores

As we have seen, the high street store evolved as cities grew from medieval times and their basic form remains surprisingly unchanged over the centuries; that is to say, ground-floor retail space with residential or commercial use above. Occasionally, the retail areas extend to upper floors or to basements, and larger stores can be formed through the amalgamation of adjacent properties. The store's façade is generally a single aspect with the storefront purposed

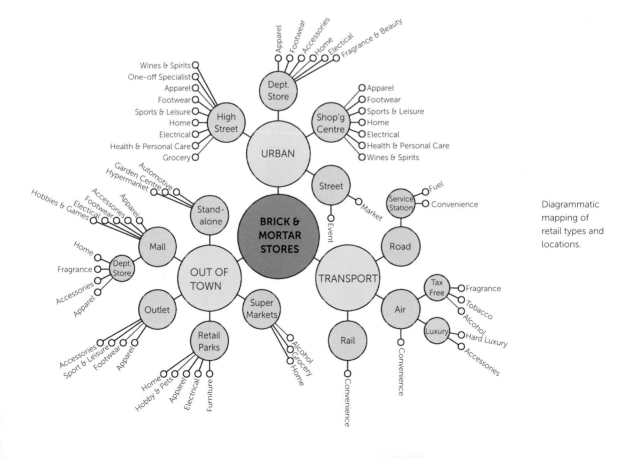

Diagrammatic mapping of retail types and locations.

to address a number of requirements, including the display of merchandise and the advertising of the store's name and nature of business as well as ensuring that the store can be secured overnight. The storefront of the high street store therefore has a lot to do and we will explore all of these requirements in future chapters. For reasons of economy, commercialism and engineering, the high street store has tended to take the form of a long rectangle with a back of house space to the rear, with limited availability of natural light, other than from the storefront.

Malls and Shopping Centres

The shopping mall as we understand it today was first developed in the US in the 1940s, although the origins of a large building containing many individual retail units can be traced much further back to the markets of the Romans and the covered bazaars of fifteenth-century Istanbul, the latter still trading today. The first mall in the modern sense, a single building with internal retail units and offering a variety of other functions, is the Lake View Store at Morgan Park in Duluth, Minnesota. This building opened in July 1916 and was designed by Chicago architects Dean & Dean. Whilst modest by today's standards, it was cutting edge in its day with the *Duluth News Tribune* reporting at the time that 'Every business concern in Morgan Park will be housed in a commodious building about 200 ft long and 100 ft wide'. When it opened it accommodated a wide variety of retail offers, including a department store, a furniture store, a grocer, a butcher and a clothing shop. As a precursor to the malls of today, Lake View Store also offered services and entertainment, and visitors could take advantage of a barber, a dentist, a pharmacy and a bank as well as a billiard hall and an auditorium. In addition, the basement contained an ice-making plant that supplied the Morgan Park area. When constructed, these various businesses were located over three floors, with access from the building's interior, although some businesses could also be located from the exterior, presumably

those on the ground floor. Lake View Store still stands today, although the building is now much altered. The upper floor has been converted to apartments and the remaining retail is now only accessible from the front of the building, so that the original form of the building as a prototype mall is now lost.

The development of the shopping mall as an out-of-town centre, disconnected from the existing urban infrastructure and reliant on shoppers arriving by car, is also seen in Minnesota at the Southdale Center at Edina on the outskirts of Minneapolis. This mall opened in 1956 and was one of the first fully enclosed and climate-controlled malls, contemporary with similar-scale developments at Valley Fair, Appleton (Wisconsin) and Northgate Mall in Seattle. Southdale was designed by Austrian émigré architect Victor Gruen, who attempted to create a retail space where the influence of weather was removed from the shopping experience and where shoppers could enjoy the experience of browsing, socializing and shopping in a comfortable and car-free environment. Gruen's vision was actually wider than the mall suggests as he had proposed a more far-reaching development including residential buildings, schools and other essential elements of a complete community along with parks and leisure facilities. As it was, only the mall was realized, and today Gruen's legacy is as the father of the suburban American mall.

It took some time before the fully fledged American-style mall found its place in the European retail market, although architect Ralph Erskine's Luleå mall, which opened in 1955, was the first fully enclosed development. Luleå is in the north of Sweden and has a sub-Arctic climate. Erskine's concern was to protect against the weather and create spaces for social interaction throughout the year; that is to say, bringing city life indoors. Despite the city having a population of only 30,000 inhabitants, when the mall opened it did indeed succeed as a focus for social interaction. As well as stores, it included a cinema and cafés. The architecture of the mall was unlike those seen in the US at the time, however, with split-level floors connected by stairs and escalators.

Contemporary postcard of Southdale Shopping Mall in Minneapolis, Minnesota, which opened in 1956.

Dubai Mall, United Arab Emirates. The modern mall is now a vital part of today's retail experience.

In the UK, shopping malls developed as smaller-scale shopping centres, often constructed as part of post-war city redevelopment; for example the Upper Precinct in Coventry which was completed in 1958 as part of the reconstruction of that heavily bombed city. Unlike the malls emerging in the US at this time, these shopping centres were not enclosed and therefore open to the elements, although always pedestrianised and with sheltered walkways offering a degree of protection. Often the shopping centre developments of this time, being significant contributors to a city's reconstruction, mixed residential use with retail (as in Coventry) or with offices, a cinema and a hotel (as at the 1964 Merrion Centre, Leeds). The development of shopping centres in the UK was furthermore the continuation of a history of enclosed and multiple unit retailing, as seen in the arcades of the Georgian age, noticeably in the UK at London's Burlington Arcade designed by the architect Samuel Ware and opened in 1819. Burlington Arcade was preceded in Europe by the arcades of Paris, Brussels and Moscow and the building form continued to develop into the Edwardian era. Today, Leeds Merrion Centre trades happily alongside the arcades of architect Frank Matcham, completed in 1904 and now part of the city's Victoria Quarter where luxury retailers trade from small units linked by glazed arcades.

In the UK, the first mall to follow the American model of a fully enclosed out-of-town development was Brent Cross in North London, opened in 1976. It comprises a two-level, 200m-long main mall with anchor department stores at both ends. Side malls connect with the mall's entrances which take advantage of the site's topography to offer access to the different internal levels from opposite sides. Right from the start, the seventy-six stores in the mall traded into the evening, which was unusual in

Frank Matcham's 1904 arcades still offer stylish shopping at the Victoria Quarter in Leeds, West Yorkshire.

1970s Britain as the norm at the time was to open stores only during regular business hours. Architecturally, Brent Cross takes its cue from American out-of-town malls, with blank external façades comprising concrete panels with ribbons of brickwork. The boxy structure, however, contains an attractive interior with top-lit natural light reaching the lower mall level thanks to the double-height central mall, with the upper level served by gallery walkways.

Thanks to town planning policies that supported urban redevelopment, shopping mall growth in the UK during the 1980s was concentrated in cities. Such was the appetite of city councils to use retail development for growth and regeneration that some eighty-five city shopping centres, each with an area of over 20,000m², were built in the UK during the decade. However, the consensus that development be focussed in city centres, primarily to protect their economic viability, was eroded during the period as free-market thinking came to inform government policy. Planning guidance on major retail development published in 1988 stated that it was not the function of the planning system to inhibit competition or preserve existing retail interests. This period coincided with the availability of out-of-town land, particularly where former heavy industrial use had now ceased: for example, Meadowhall in South Yorkshire, which opened in September 1990, was developed on land vacated by the steel industry. That same year, Lakeside in Thurrock, Essex, opened on the site of a former chalk quarry. The size of these mall developments, supported with cinemas, restaurants and other leisure activities, allowed them to draw on vast catchment areas. Whilst the number of out-of-town enclosed malls constructed was low and no more than half a dozen were built with a floor area of over 100,000m², their impact on traditional city centres could be very negative. Traditional retail sites in city centres, suffering from traffic congestion, limits on car parking capacity and an inhospitable British climate, were seen as second best by mall-shoppers who flocked to enclosed, safe and car-friendly malls. The balance between urban and out-of-town development was finally redressed in 1996 when Planning Policy Guidance Note 6 set out to prioritize the vitality and viability of city centres. Further legislation since has made new out-of-town mall developments unlikely in the coming years, although most are continuing to expand and to offer a better mix of high-end stores and increased leisure opportunities.

The malls that were developed subsequently are better integrated into both the architectural grain of the city and its commercial life. Architecturally, we have seen the continuation of enclosed mall building, such as Westfield London, to developments with extensive open-air shopping streets such as Liverpool One. Both developments opened in 2008 with Westfield London's sister mall at Stratford, East London, opening three years later.

Retail Parks

The development of retail parks in the UK runs alongside that of out-of-town shopping malls, as much of their growth was a consequence of changes in planning legislation. In the late 1970s, out-of-town superstores and large-format retail sheds began to be built. From a town planning perspective, it was felt that these forms of retail, dependent as they were on large floor plates and vast swathes of car parking, was better located beyond or at the edge of the city centre. Development was controlled through an assessment of calculated need based on prediction and using census data collected by the local authority. This effectively acted as a cap on development, as once the need for a store had been met, no further stores of the same type would be granted consent. The removal of this cap was lifted in the 1980s, and indeed as early as 1981 local authorities had ceased collecting commercial census data. The same 1988 planning guidance on major retail development that ignited the development of malls encouraged development that might relieve pressure on city centres, particularly where new development sites could be found on brownfield or derelict land. Today there are over 1,200 out-of-town retail parks in the UK, many comprising DIY stores, furniture warehouses and other big-box retail uses. In the US in the 1980s a new concept was developed, known as the outlet centre. These centres are fashion-led and offer discounted merchandise that is end-of-line stock or surplus. The concept arrived in the UK in 1995 when McArthur Glen opened Cheshire Oaks in the north-west of England. Outlet centres have seen an increasing slice of market share since and at the time of writing there are now around forty-eight outlet centres in the UK, of which around two-thirds are out-of-town. As the concept has developed, some outlet centres have focussed on luxury, with targeted marketing aimed at visiting tourists, such as Bicester Village, which offers over 160 designer brands. As the market has matured, operators have introduced more and better food and beverage offers to give the outlet centres greater appeal. The stores themselves do not offer the latest collections, nor charge full price, and the store interiors reflect this, often being pared-down versions of the original brand concept.

Department Stores

Bon Marché in Paris is acknowledged to have been the original department store, although some general stores and drapers' businesses in other parts of the world pre-date Bon Marché and also evolved into what we recognize as department stores today. Bon Marché was founded by Aristide Boucicaut in 1852 and was established on the principle of large scale, allowing keen pricing, as well as a wide variety of merchandise which was, as the name suggests, organized into departments. Prices were fixed and the merchandise on offer designed to appeal to all socio-economic groups. The inspiration behind the department stores' impressive staging of the time was undoubtedly the great exhibitions and world fairs that were held in these years. In Paris, Bon Marché was followed by the establishment of other famous names such as

Printemps (1865), Galeries Lafayette (1895) and Samaritaine which moved to a purpose-built store in 1910. Paris was perhaps a natural location in which the department store could develop: not only was it a teeming commercial city of almost three million citizens, but it was also the centre of Europe's artistic and cultural life and particularly fashion and couture during the Belle Époque.

The department store as a concept took root in the US during this era, no doubt inspired by the Parisian examples. Macy's was founded in New York in 1858 and Bloomingdale's three years later in the same city. Wanamaker's of Philadelphia, founded in 1876, can also lay claim to being one of America's first true department stores, with innovations such as electric lighting and fixed and tagged pricing (in an era when haggling persisted). The industrial might of the US in the early twentieth century was reflected in the founding of new retail businesses not just in New York but across the country. Examples include Marshall Field of Chicago, Illinois (1881), J.C. Penney of Kemmerer, Wyoming (1902) and Nieman Marcus, founded in Dallas, Texas (1907). During the latter half of the twentieth century, many regional department stores were amalgamated into larger groups, which became nationwide brands. Kohl's, America's largest group today, comprises over 1,150 stores, most of these in suburban shopping malls, mirroring the general

Neiman Marcus department store interior from the short-lived Hudson Yards store, New York.

migration from downtown locations to the mall that began in the 1960s.

Many of London's department stores evolved from other businesses such as drapery or dry goods that were trading in the early part of the nineteenth century. Harrods grew from a grocery business established by Charles Henry Harrod in London in 1824, but it wasn't until 1905 and under new ownership that the famous Brompton Road store opened. London's grandest and most famous store of this era was Whiteleys, founded in 1863 and moving to its Queensway site in 1911. Whilst Harrods and Whiteleys had evolved piecemeal until acquiring sites large enough to accommodate new bespoke stores, Selfridges was established in London as a fully fledged department store from its inception. Harry Gordon Selfridge opened the first phase of his department store on London's Oxford Street in 1909. He knew the retail business from Marshall Field and Company in Chicago, where he had risen to the position of junior partner. On visiting London, Selfridge recognized a gap in the market, not only in terms of the grandeur and scale of the stores, but in the customer service that was offered. The speed at which Selfridge developed his store was impressive, the first phase being built and opened within three years of his London visit. The store design always envisaged the classical frontage that runs along Oxford Street between Orchard Street and Duke Street, although

Selfridge Building, Oxford Street, London.

1909 postcard issued by Selfridge & Co., London, showing the original department store before it was extended along Oxford Street.

it took a further twenty years to acquire the remaining parcels of land and complete the architectural concept. Selfridge employed a team of architects to realize his vision, including Daniel Burnham of Chicago who had worked for Marshall Field and designed the Wanamaker store in Philadelphia. Burnham employed a steel-frame method of construction, familiar in the US but unknown in the UK in the early 1900s. Its use in Selfridge's building led to a change in the London building regulations, such was its novelty.

In the same way that the shopping mall as a location features in much of today's fiction, from *Dawn of the Dead* (1978) to *Better Call Saul* (2015), so the department store reflected the commerce and culture of the first half of the twentieth century, for example in the Marx Brothers' *The Big Store* (1941) and *Miracle on 34th Street* (1947), the latter of which was filmed on location in Macy's New York. In the UK, Norman Wisdom starred in the 1953 *Trouble In Store*. What is it that gave department stores this cultural significance? Whether in New York, London, Paris or Tokyo, the size of the stores and the architectural statement to which they aspired are common themes. The department store magnates of the Edwardian era built big and so their stores became landmarks. Stores with floor areas over 20,000m^2 were not uncommon, with many stores occupying whole city blocks which thus allowed for long runs of display windows at street level. As we have seen in the example of Gordon Selfridge, department stores were at the forefront of technical innovation but equally they allowed a retail culture to develop which was female-friendly, providing respectable places for women to shop, socialize and be seen. It is estimated that as many as 85 per cent of the department store's Edwardian era customers were female. At a time when public conveniences were rare and overwhelmingly male-dominated, it is particularly significant that department stores provided female toilets that were easily accessed and safe. Freed from the necessity to limit time away from the home, women were able to visit, stay and shop, while enjoying the lounges, tea rooms and music events that stores provided.

The open layout of the department store, which allowed customers to browse and to touch the merchandise, was in contrast to the proprietor-managed trade of the previous century, typified by the salesperson standing guard over a counter. Over the years department stores have sought to offer both bargain goods sold cheaply alongside luxury and exclusive goods that promote their standing. In parallel with this mix, designed to appeal to the widest market, department stores took on promotional activities of the like never before seen in the retail world. These live on to this day in the art of the window display, the in-store book signing or the celebrity product launch. In the early 1900s, however, department store visitors might have been entertained by the store's orchestra, art exhibitions or stunts such as the landing of an aeroplane on the roof, as happened at Galeries Lafayette in Paris in 1919.

If the early years of the twentieth century represented the golden age of the department store, it does not mean that retailers have not continued to explore and develop the format. The world's largest department store, Shinsegae in Busan, South Korea, dwarfs its Edwardian ancestors with its 300,000m^2 size. Many of Europe's leading department stores have passed the centenary of their founding and have gone on to instigate major programmes of renewal and expansion, amongst them KaDeWe in Berlin, Selfridges in London and La Samaritaine in Paris.

Store-in-Store Retail

Today's department store is a carefully curated blend of 'own bought' or store-branded merchandise and externally branded retail that has its own identity on the retail floor. The idea that brands could trade from their own space within the department store has its origins in the Henri Bendel store, founded in New York in the late 1890s. Bendel's store sold women's apparel, fragrances, accessories and cosmetics. The retail offer was a blend of Bendel's own products and external brands. In the 1970s, this approach crystallized into

a 'street of shops', a concept developed by the store's president at the time, Geraldine Stutz. Her approach was subsequently copied and adapted and is today seen in department stores around the world. Department stores endeavour to retain the sense that the customer is still visiting a unique place, with its character, history and house style, and take care to ensure that they do not become a mall-like container for brands. In order to achieve this, brands are usually required to work to store guidelines to ensure that the department store's vision for their retail space is respected.

Transport Hubs

Travellers are today familiar with the concentration of retail in airports. The origins of this lie in duty-free shopping, whereby goods purchased are exempt from local sales tax or duties provided they are sold to travellers leaving the country. Duty-free offers tend to be highly taxed consumables such as alcohol and tobacco, although fragrances, cosmetics, electronics, luxury fashion and accessories are now strongly represented. The first airport to launch duty-free shopping was Shannon in Ireland. As northern Europe's most westerly airport, Shannon was ideally placed to serve the developing air routes between Europe and the US. In the 1940s, Shannon was not only a transatlantic gateway but also served as a refuelling stop for flights originating or returning to other countries in Europe. Shannon's duty-free shop was launched in 1947, just two years after receiving its first scheduled commercial flight. In Europe, duty-free shopping grew in all major airports, with the planning of airports changing to recognize the needs of retail. In 1999, duty-free shopping for travellers within the European Union ceased. This was a logical extension of the single market which made the notion of import or export between European member countries redundant. Duty-free prices were still available to travellers leaving the European Union, but for the majority of shoppers travelling through Europe's airports, tax-free shopping had ended. By the late 1990s, it was also clear that sales tax alone was not

Transport hubs are now home to many retail outlets like FatFace at Waterloo Station, London.

South Korea and Dubai International, each turned over in excess of $2 billion.

Temporary Retail and Kiosks

This group of retail encompasses pop-up stores, kiosks and other temporary stores that brands occasionally might use in lieu of a fully fledged store. This can arise out of practical necessity (for example, when a temporary site is needed because of refurbishment or relocation) or it can be to test a new concept. Brands considering a mall or transport hub location might occupy a kiosk site for a period of time to test the market and establish the location's viability before committing to a permanent unit. Kiosks can also be introduced for specific seasonal trade or related to events. The main design considerations in planning kiosk locations are the limits on space, usually meaning a much reduced offer, and the 360-degree visibility that the kiosk enjoys. Kiosks are ideally made to be easy to build from prefabricated parts to allow overnight installation and quick dismantling. Consideration should be given to how the kiosk is to be reused or adapted in future locations.

Pop-up stores have become an important branch of store design. At the established end of the market, they allow brands to experiment with new, more radical design concepts, perhaps in direct contravention of the brand's cherished standards. Because pop-up stores have a limited life and a more extrovert design stance, they are great for brand promotion and as a conduit to new demographics in the market. Because of the temporary nature of pop-up stores, they are likely to be constructed quickly and cheaply whilst making a strong design statement.

the only factor to influence a product's price. Competitors based outside the airport, or increasingly online, who did not have to carry the overheads required to trade from an airport, could offer similar or lower prices on many goods. This led to a reinvention of the retail offer in European airports, with a greater focus on luxury goods to tempt the impulse buyer and an attempt to build retail offers around a sense of place and occasion. For luxury retailers, this has made the airport one of the most important markets in which to trade and the new airport terminals of the last two decades have included vast areas of retail, equivalent in size to a small city mall. Heathrow Terminal 5, which opened in 2008, is home to more than fifty stores. One of the reasons cited for the long delay in opening Berlin Brandenburg Willy Brandt Airport was the necessity to increase the terminal size to accommodate sufficient retail. It was reported that the airport's operating company anticipated earning half of all revenues through retail sales.

Elsewhere in the world we have seen a similar development of airport retail, with luxury at the heart of the airport operators' offer. In 2018, the world's two largest duty-free airports, Incheon International in

The Abercrombie & Fitch
moose finds expression
in the brand's Kids Store.

Chapter Two

Store Planning

MARCUS VITRUVIUS POLLIO, THE ROMAN architect, suggested that 'firmness, commodity and delight' were the three defining qualities of a well-designed building. These same qualities can be found in well-planned and constructed retail space where we find robust construction and functional planning carried off with a design aesthetic that excites and delights the visitor. The store designer's role is to ensure that these considerations are given appropriate weight. After all, what purpose is served in designing an exquisite and enticing store from which it is impossible to sell enough product to keep the retailer's business viable, or where the beautiful finishes lack the durability demanded in a busy store and require constant and expensive maintenance?

The store designer must therefore strike a balance between many influences on the design, from project constraints to the retailer's desire to promote their brand or business through store design. As retail's built environment increasingly moves towards offering the customer an experience-led visit to the store, store design is moving away from a depository of goods to browse to a physical manifestation of the brand experience, itself part of an omnichannel presentation of the brand, designed to reinforce our understanding of and our appreciation of the brand. Where successfully executed and curated, the well-designed store becomes a vital weapon in a brand's armoury for winning and influencing customers.

Retail to intrigue and delight. Louis Vuitton at the Dubai Mall, United Arab Emirates.

THE STORE DESIGNER'S BRIEF

Brand Storytelling

Before embarking on the design of a retail space, time should be spent on capturing the brief. A well-thought out brief is the foundation of a successful project and should capture the aspirations of the project, whilst recognizing the constraints. Some elements of the brief, such as the aesthetic direction and brand storytelling, might be expressed through mood boards whereas capacity and product range can be expressed through hard data.

The constraints on a project might be budgetary or time-critical, requiring the store to open at a fixed time in order to take advantage of an important event or to coincide with a particular season. The location, shape and size of the site are also very significant constraints.

The brief should be recorded in writing and supplemented with sketches, numbers, mood boards or whatever best captures the aspiration of the project. We shall explore the project design and delivery cycle later, but in this chapter we will look at the design process.

It is no accident that the grid of benches in an Apple store reminds us of a pristine laboratory, or that Louboutin seek to capture the intimacy of the private apartment in their stores. The design of the store reflects the brand's culture, tells the brand's story and is vital in promoting the brand to the customer and potential customer. In some cases, the store becomes instantly recognizable from its aesthetic, barely requiring a name over the door. Telling the brand's story and reflecting its culture does not, however, mean that the design is frozen thereafter. Brands periodically review and refresh their store designs as they evolve or as they seek to appeal to a different segment of the market or a new demographic. If the store is indeed the physical manifestation of the brand, what are the important messages conveyed? The answer to this is unique to each brand but is likely to contain aspects of several themes.

Brand storytelling at Nike House of Innovation, New York.

Brand History

As customers we are curious about the origins of a brand, whether very long-standing companies who trace their origins back three hundred years like Fortnum & Mason or recent start-ups carving out a niche for themselves.

Community Creation

Loyalty to a brand is a very powerful path to sales and is driven by strong relationships with the customer. The idea that customers belong to a community and that a store's design reflects this has gained traction over recent years, very obviously in the cases of cycle clothing brand Rapha, who brand their stores as club-houses, or Nespresso, who offer tiers of membership based on customers' loyalty to the brand.

Aspiration

The quality of the store should reflect the quality and price point of the merchandise on sale. Presenting high-value products against a low-quality backdrop presents a high psychological barrier to sales.

Storytelling

Trust in a brand comes from a knowledge of the brand's origins, the motivations of its founders, its attitude to sustainability and its quality. References to these messages can be subtle, to be read by those with a keen eye for the brand, or as explicit as the moose of Abercrombie Kids.

Nespresso fosters customer loyalty through their *Nespresso & You* programme.

CASE STUDY: BRAND STORYTELLING AT 10 CORSO COMO, MILAN

The entrance to 10 Corso Como, Milan. (Photo: 10 Corso Como)

10 Corso Como was opened by Carla Sozzani in 1991 in the Porta Nuova neighbourhood of Milan. The store occupies an interesting and possibly unlikely site, comprising a former car garage and a traditional Milanese palazzo. The palazzo's architecture of single rooms linked by common circulation space, is arranged around a courtyard which visitors enter through a narrow entrance from the street. The store's name is simply the building's address, which is picked out in mosaic using the brand's distinctive graphics above the main door. 10 Corso Como started out as a gallery with an emphasis on photography, in Sozzani's view an overlooked medium in the art world at the time. To reach the gallery on the second floor, visitors crossed the garage area, but by 1997 this business had vacated so that the whole site could gradually be developed. The large industrial space, combined with the palazzo's traditional rooms, allowed new activities to flourish to include a book store and a publishing company; then came a café that expanded into a restaurant, the store itself, and finally a small boutique hotel designed by American artist and Sozzani's partner Kris Ruhs. The courtyard supports a garden, now recognized for its role in offering a haven to visiting migratory birds.

Courtyard garden in the heart of 10 Corso Como, Milan. (Photo: 10 Corso Como)

Carla Sozzani had been a magazine editor before opening the store and 10 Corso Como almost feels like a magazine come to life, with a variety of experiences carefully curated under the editor's watchful eye. As she herself said, 'I made 10 Corso Como because editing is the only thing I really like to do.' The sensual experience we feel when visiting 10 Corso Como is the intention and foundation of the brand, where culture takes centre stage, supported by the commercial activity of the brand. The Italian slow food movement was in its infancy when the store first opened, but 10 Corso Como's attitude to retailing reflected this mood. The customer is in an environment where slow shopping prevails. The design of the store and its range of attractions let the visitor know that they should find time to browse, to enjoy the galleries and the garden as well as the store.

Retail space created from a former industrial building at 10 Corso Como, Milan. (Photo: 10 Corso Como)

The Bookshop at 10 Corso Como, Milan. (Photo: 10 Corso Como)

Sozzani's 10 Corso Como was pioneering as a culture-led and curated retail store. This type of retail, now known as a concept store, is not primarily focussed on selling products, but rather sells a cultural experience or a lifestyle, of which retail contributes only a part. As magazines change and seek out new and interesting insights for their readers, so the concept store is constantly refreshed and new for the visitor.

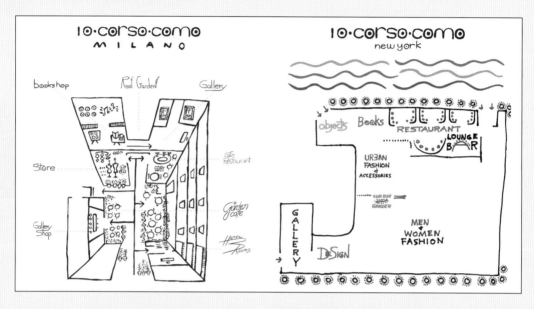

Concept plans of the 10 Corso Como stores in Milan and Fulton Market, New York. (Photo: 10 Corso Como)

10 Corso Como expanded the brand beyond Milan and at one time had outposts in Shanghai, Beijing and New York. The New York store, which was located in the Seaport district's Fulton Market, sadly closed in April 2020, a victim of a tough economic climate brought about by the coronavirus pandemic. The design of the store nevertheless remains an interesting example of how the original brand design, developed organically and piecemeal in Milan, could serve as the idea for a new store concept in New York.

Entrance to 10 Corso Como, Fulton Market, New York.

The Seaport building is a former fish market and so the parallels between the re-purposing of a former car garage and an old market hall are obvious. Both offer large volume spaces, and this is exploited in New York, where an open-plan design allows all of the store's offers to live within a single space. The strength of the Seaport's existing architecture is what attracted Carla Sozzani and Kris Ruhs to the site, as was the chance to grow through culture and commerce in an interesting and changing community.

The interior architecture of a newly created store inevitably differs from one that grew organically, but there is more than a nod of recognition to Milan in the Fulton Market store. The floors are an element of which Carla Sozzani is particularly proud. Kris Ruhs began exploring the applications of coloured polished cement thirty years ago in New York for Norma Kamali's commercial spaces. It can be modified for a variety of interiors, both residential and commercial, allowing sweeping visual changes with no physical disruption necessary. It can change as often as the client wishes it to. Once a year, they have been all changed and renovated by Ruhs with slightly different new nuances, from green to purple, or to light blue.

Floating light fittings in the interior of 10 Corso Como, Fulton Market, New York.

Electric display at 10 Corso Como, Fulton Market, New York.

The lighting itself in NYC was designed and constructed under Ruhs' direction with recycled glass. The requirement was to illuminate what is in reality a low ceiling by creating a visual lily pad effect of soft light elements across a broad expanse floating in darkness; this helped to create the illusion of depth above, as though looking into a dark pond.

Areas of the store defined through screens and backdrops at 10 Corso Como, Fulton Market, New York.

The courtyard garden of Milan cannot be replicated in New York, but that does not mean that the store design wasn't influenced by the natural world. In the summer the store was surrounded with bushes and tables for the outdoor café. Inside, and at the heart of the store, was a 'tank' filled with real sea grasses in ceramic pots designed by Ruhs. The other elements found their way into the store through sight and sound as 10 Corso Como is a concept that engages all the senses. This included curated and customized music as well as the fish ceramics incorporated into the architecture. The attention shown to the exquisite presentation boxes, shopping bags, papers, ribbons, all of which carried the store's logo, allowed the spirit of the whole store to be captured in a single detail.

Beautifully detailed cash wrap area at 10 Corso Como, Fulton Market, New York.

The spirit of the whole store captured in a single detail at 10 Corso Como, Fulton Market, New York.

As a curated store, it was important that Corso Como 10's New York store introduced the local market to its Italian heritage, as well as reflecting the local scene. At Fulton Market, some of the brands so cherished by Sozzani in Milan – Alaïa, Gucci, Ferragamo, Margiela, Matsuda, Comme des Garçons, Moncler – were showcased. The café was, of course, Italian and with a nod back to the brand's origins the bookshop's focus was on photography and art. Visitors to 10 Corso Como, whether in Milan or New York, sought what the brand describes as 'an experience that is pleasing to themselves or pleasing to those they love'. That doesn't mean that each store need be the same. On the contrary, every place has its own *genius loci* and the successful store, particularly one that carries the ethos of culture and curation, should acknowledge this. Sadly, we will not now see how the Fulton Market site would have developed and responded to New York's shifting cultural influences. We can at least still take pleasure from the eclectic original that is Milan.

STORE PLANNING AND THE CUSTOMER JOURNEY

The internal planning of the store must consider the circulation route through the retail spaces within. We must also consider how this route links the goods on display and connects those parts of the store that service and support the customers' needs, such as the point of sale or fitting rooms. Circulation routes and the sequence in which these elements are encountered are often described as the customer journey and its importance is recognized in creating a mood, enticing impulse buys, encouraging sales and telling the brand's story. The customer journey is how the customer experiences the store from the point of entry, through their navigation of the store's interior, to their experience of the merchandise, to point of sale and exit.

Threshold

From the first view of the storefront, the customer may feel curiosity, excitement, anticipation, reassurance or perhaps even dread. The store's threshold can provide the first clues as to the brand's essential qualities and values.

Contrast, for example, a typical open mall threshold, providing easy and relaxed access to the store. The young customer recognizes that there is no bar to entry, and that the mood is relaxed. A store that creates a strong bar to casual entry, perhaps with a closed door and a limited view of what lies beyond, is signalling to potential customers that access is exclusive.

Entrance Area

In his book *Why We Buy*, Paco Underhill observed that shoppers just crossing the store's threshold often overlooked shopping baskets that were available immediately inside the door. He formulated the theory that the customer's focus on entering the store is directly ahead, seeking out visual clues to the store's layout and product offers. He termed this area the 'decompression zone' and it is worthy of recognition. The store planner should accept that the customer's attention as they enter the store is elsewhere and the layout should recognize this, allowing customers to acclimatize to the store's interior.

Within any store are fixed points, like villages in the landscape, that customers need to identify and reach as part of their journey.

Display

The display of goods and visual merchandising can take a bewildering variety of forms but essentially

This threshold carries a vibrant statement of MAC's brand values at Hudson Yards, New York.

Time and space to decompress. Kate Spade at Hudson Yards, New York.

Candy boxes displayed as desirable objects by Sugarfina, New York.

breaks down to perimeter display, designed to be seen from one side only, or free-standing displays designed to be experienced in the round. The design of display is usually driven by the nature of the goods contained but other influences on display methods are ergonomics, product density and material aesthetics.

Within the store are key non-display elements that the customer should be able to identify and locate with ease. These include customer service areas, lifts and stairs and, in larger stores, entrance points to adjacent departments.

Point of Sale

This is the traditionally the till where customers make payment and have purchases de-tagged, wrapped and bagged. It is important that customers can easily identify the point of sale within a large retail floor. Customers will generally be generous with their time when browsing and selecting but demand a prompt and efficient sales transaction when ready to leave. The same attitude prevails with self-checkout points of sale, where complicated and error-prone systems leave the customer with a poor impression of the store. Fixed points of sale are no longer a necessity due to technologies such as asset tagging which allows

registered customers to purchase without the physical act of transaction. Where stores seek a closer interaction with customers, mobile sales tools, typically tablet-based, mean that transactions can be made anywhere in the store, thus lessening the significance of a fixed point of sale counter.

Returns, Click and Collect, Enquiries

Many larger stores recognize that segregating sales from these other functions allows specific customer needs to be addressed without interfering with sales transactions. The position of returns and click and collect in the store is very often determined by adjacency to the back of house as both functions require access to the stockroom or product-holding area. Enquiry desks, or simply an identifiable sales associate, should, however, be located close to the entrance.

Fitting Rooms

Where apparel is sold, the store should provide fitting rooms, allowing customers to try on clothes to check for size, fit and style. Just as the product density in the

Designed with the needs of the customer in mind. Child's fitting room at Abercrombie Kids, Willowbrook Mall, Wayne, New Jersey.

store reflects a particular price point, so do the number and size of the fitting rooms. The fast fashion retailer with a young target market will be satisfied with a high number of small, functional fitting rooms whereas the haute couture brand understands the importance of larger, more comfortable fitting rooms, allowing space for the customer to be assisted with fitting. Whatever the store's place in the market, consideration should be given to the specific needs of the customer, including larger fitting rooms in children's stores to allow an adult to accompany a child, or fitting rooms designed to address the needs of disabled customers.

Vertical Circulation

This is the collective name for all the means by which customers travel between different floors in the store, most commonly stairs and lifts but also escalators and ramps. The wait for the lift or the physical effort of climbing the stairs are known to be strong disincentives to customers exploring the store beyond their immediate location. It is not uncommon for larger stores to provide a single escalator from the ground to the first floor (and often near the store's entrance) for which there is no return escalator. In this case the weary customer is expected to find the staircase and walk down. In department stores and malls,

Well-appointed fitting rooms reflecting a high level of customer service at Chanel, München. (Photo: Hyphen)

the location and direction of escalators are carefully planned to ensure that customers are encouraged to easily reach other floors.

Escalators demand a large footprint, and in many cases there is either insufficient space to install them, or at least a reluctance to sacrifice sales area. Many retailers have instead sought to make a virtue of the staircase and in many contemporary designs, the stairway is one of the most interesting parts of the store to see and experience. Store designers and engineers have created ever more elegant and technically ambitious stair designs and it not uncommon for a store design to be remembered for this as much as its display windows. In larger stores, the stairs can provide the vantage point from which the store can be seen and understood.

Carefully considered vertical circulation at Emporia Mall in Malmö, Sweden. Each core is coloured differently to aid orientation.

The staircase is central to the customer journey at Nike House of Innovation, New York.

Where lifts are provided, this is often first and foremost to serve customers unable to take advantage of the stairs. Lifts should therefore be sized to accommodate wheelchair users and parents with children in prams or buggies. Technical constraints, and particularly those imposed by existing buildings, generally mean that lift speeds are low and offer little of interest to the customer. However, where a combination of space and height allows the creation of an atrium or large void, glass-faced lifts can be used with dramatic effect.

Product groups excellently organised and differentiated at Abercrombie & Fitch, Eston Town Center, Ohio.

Product Groups

The internal arrangement of the store may be open, encouraging customers to explore the space in an unplanned and unregulated way, allowing them to make their own discoveries. Alternatively, the internal store planning may strictly and very obviously set out to identify the customer areas that are gender-specific or concerned with the retail of a specific group of products. If the designer intends to emphasize the differences in products on display, then 'rooms within rooms' might be an appropriate device to create separate sales areas, focussing on a particular customer's needs. Where a large retail space contains many varieties of product groups, signage to guide the customer takes on a greater significance.

Store Layouts

It is useful to consider the variety of strategies when planning the internal layout of the store. Not only will the layout determine how the retail space is experienced and used by shoppers, but it will determine how products are presented in the store. To some degree, the layout will affect how the stores services, including lighting, are planned and installed. We can also understand the store layout in terms of the customer journey or route through the space and ask ourselves what might draw a customer deeper into the store. How convenient is it for the customer to find what they are looking for and how easily can we delight them and tempt them into an impulse purchase?

Store layout options to suit different product densities and circulation preferences.

It would be a mistake to think that the answers to these questions remain the same for all. The journey through the store for a regular visitor will very likely be different from the customer journey of a someone who is exploring the space for the first time. In the past this understanding came from observation and the retailer's intuition and experience; these are valuable skills which can today be supported by analytics based on real-time data gathered in the store. The strategies for store planning are rarely translated directly into layouts as the real-world constraints of existing buildings come to bear, and designs might have elements of more than one strategy, particularly on larger sites.

Aisle and Mat

The walkways are clearly demarcated and usually there is a strict design regime that keeps product and visual merchandising display off the walkway. This is typically found in large stores and particularly department stores, allowing customers to easily transition from one area of the store to another. Aisle and mat layouts allow each mat to have its own identity in terms of product line, range or brand. Brand fit-outs on mats might use very different finishes and so department stores endeavour to unify the overall retail environment through common floor, ceiling and wall finishes.

Loop

A loop layout works well when the store's offer comprises product on mid-floor and perimeter fixtures and good densities can be achieved. The store is, however, imposing a limited choice of journeys on the customer, which can make the sequence in which product is encountered seem contrived.

Front to Back Aisle

This is an arrangement that is often suitable for smaller stores, with a single aisle between the entrance area and the point of sale. This allows the store to be easily read and understood by the customer.

Grid

This structured layout creates clearly delineated areas of display and walkway; it is best suited to predominantly low-height display so as to preserve sight lines and avoid a forest of fixtures.

Dinsko use front to back aisle space planning to create a strong sense of order at Täby Mall, Stockholm.

Free Form or Random

When used with very high-density display, random or apparently unstructured layouts can be very unappealing as they appear as thoughtless collections of products with no curation behind their merchandising. However, when placed in low density with interest points that draw the customer into the store, they can be effective in displaying product whilst remaining flexible as the range changes.

Linked Rooms

The ethos of this layout is to create separate rooms, usually of a domestic scale, which are presented as a formal sequence of spaces, perhaps in the style of a grand house. The customer journey centres around exploring the rooms to discover the merchandise and display in each. Because the degree of design control is high, the flexibility that results can be disadvantageous. Linked rooms allow, for example,

Random planning is overlaid with a careful ordering of the fixture heights to create a landscape of product at M&G, Beijing.

A room within a room is subtly created with a grid-like mesh at Forty Five Ten, Hudson Yards, New York.

dedicated areas for men, women and children within the same store.

The arrangement of separate rooms can create an interesting journey through the store, ideally with something of interest to encourage the customer to explore further. Sight lines, the use of natural light where possible and the avoidance of back-tracking across larger floor plates all help to hold the customer's interest.

Gallery

This is usually a minimalist approach, where the small number of products are presented as would-be art in a gallery; this can be a useful layout for pop-up stores or experimental temporary spaces where there is less of a requirement for dense merchandising.

This tube-shaped store by Irvins in Macao suggests an art installation, with its all-black décor and bold graphic dominating the store.

CASE STUDY: THE PSYCHOLOGY OF SHOPPING AT STANSTED AIRPORT

On the macro level, particularly in the mall or the airport, greater emphasis has evolved on controlling the customers' paths through the retail space. When the present-day Stansted Airport terminal was opened in 1991, it was conceived by its architect Norman Foster as a single space, albeit an enormous one with a volume of 600,000m³. The architect's concept envisaged a very simple form of way-finding for travellers, with an easy understanding of their location as they could see for themselves the four enclosing walls of the terminal and what lay ahead. The retail spaces were enclosed in single-storey cabins, standing in the middle of the terminal as independent 'buildings within buildings'. Whilst such a design facilitated the traveller's journey from arrival to boarding gate, I suspect that it discouraged visitors to explore the retail offer, one that would have relied on both backtracking and the prospect of taking unnecessary and potentially unrewarding steps away from the principal traffic route.

■	Duty Free
■	Retail Units
■	Food & Beverage Units
□	Public Circulation

Stansted Airport duty-free shopping, retail and food and beverage zones enclose the route connecting travellers to their departure gates.

From 1997 the airport saw a rapid rise in passenger numbers, driven by the rise of budget airlines connecting the UK to the rest of Europe. In 2015 the airport's owner, Manchester Airports Group, revamped the terminal to streamline check-in and security, the former reducing in size to reflect the changing nature of air travel, with most passengers now checking-in online. The airside retail offer was increased by over 10,000m² including food and beverage offers. The passenger route through the retail area has been designed to counter the instinct to walk in as direct a line as possible and choice is removed from the traveller by means of an indirect, snaking path from the airside entry point of the security check to the departure point of the gate, or at least the lounge prior to the gate. The path curves to the left, meaning that the traveller is walking anti-clockwise. It has been hypothesized that as the majority of people are right-handed and pull rolling luggage with their right hand, this causes them to walk along an anti-clockwise path whilst looking to their right: as a result, this theory predicts that higher sales are generated if more space and merchandise are available to the visitors' right.

The path through is clearly delineated and the brands within announce their presence with strong signage that is hard not to notice. World Duty Free, Stansted Airport.

This snaking path allows all twenty-six retail units to display their storefronts to potential customers along the route and the route also snakes through an open-plan duty-free area, exposing the potential customer to potential impulse buys. The fostering of potential impulse spending is reinforced through an extensive use of demonstrations, tastings and promotional activities. The snaking pathway to the lounge increases travellers' journeys five-fold and is in all likelihood a welcome distraction for passengers with time to kill, although less valuable to those running to their departure gates. Within the space, signage is obvious and explicit, leaving little for the architecture to contribute to intuitive way-finding: thus the contemporary Stansted has become the very antithesis of Norman Foster's vision. Where faced with choice along the route, for example to turn and browse the duty-free display, the principal route is strongly delineated with changes in floor colour. Stansted's highly controlled layout essentially offers the traveller no choice, other than to pass through the duty-free shop and then past all of the individual retailers in turn. This arrangement denies the possibility for the traveller to seek a direct route to the lounge or their gate and ensures that the entire retail offer can be seen and understood without the need to choose paths or backtrack.

SPACE PLANNING ERGONOMICS

From a practical point of view, the layout of internal walls and furniture must respect certain minimum dimensions, which may also be reinforced by statutory code requirements or building regulations in respect of wheelchair access or minimum fire escape routes.

shopping centre was long ago established by developers at 30 feet or 9.13m from face of store to face of store. Over the years, this has become a less rigid rule of thumb as mall design has evolved from the linear or T-shaped plan. A wider aisle, allowing for a greater height of galleried space and the installation of mid-aisle kiosks, has seen the width increase so that 11m and upwards are now more common.

Aisle Widths and Circulation

Very Wide

Applicable to larger-scale and mall developments, the pedestrian circulation width within a mall or

Wide

In department stores, principal circulation routes should be wide enough to allow the passing of groups of people without encroaching on the adjacent retail space. Typically, as much as 2.4m should be allowed

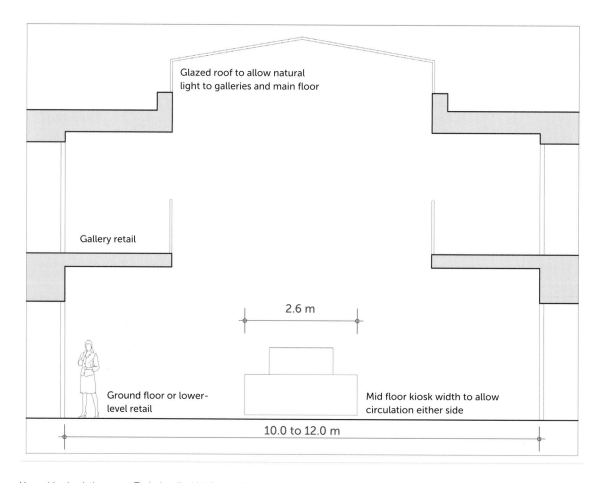

Glazed roof to allow natural light to galleries and main floor

Gallery retail

2.6 m

Ground floor or lower-level retail

Mid floor kiosk width to allow circulation either side

10.0 to 12.0 m

Very wide circulation route. Typical mall width for top-lit, double-storey configuration.

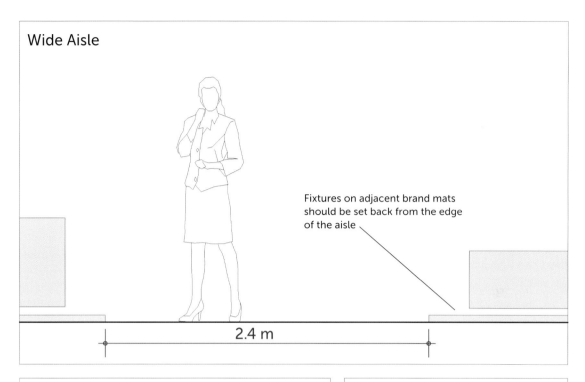

Wide Aisle

Fixtures on adjacent brand mats should be set back from the edge of the aisle

2.4 m

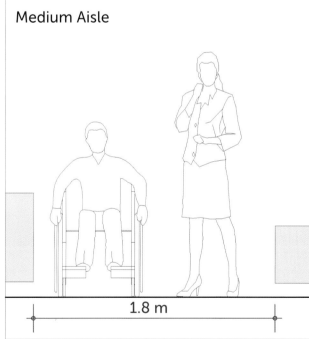

Medium Aisle

1.8 m

Narrow Aisle

1.2 m

Standard aisle widths allowing for differing densities of circulation.

for wide aisles. Where retail mats are demarcated along the route of the aisle it is useful to allow a small amount of separation between display fixtures and the edge of the aisle: this allows customers to step off the aisle to browse the display.

Medium

In most stores this is the minimum requirement for the principal circulation route connecting the entrance, point of sale, vertical circulation points and so on. A width of 1.8m not only allows small groups of customers to circulate in comfort but also allows two wheelchair users or children's buggies to pass safely.

Narrow

Whilst there may be instances where a narrower aisle is needed or cannot be avoided, there is a diminishing return in reducing the aisle in order to achieve a denser display of product. Aisles that are too narrow are not conducive to browsing, forcing the customer to jostle for position or to turn back when the aisle is

Hierarchy of aisle widths well illustrated at Uniqlo, Hudson Yards, New York.

congested. A minimum of 1.2m should be sought for narrow aisles, not least because this is the minimum width in which a wheelchair user can manoeuvre with freedom.

Reach and Browse Heights

At best, display heights that are either too low or too high will discourage shoppers from reaching or

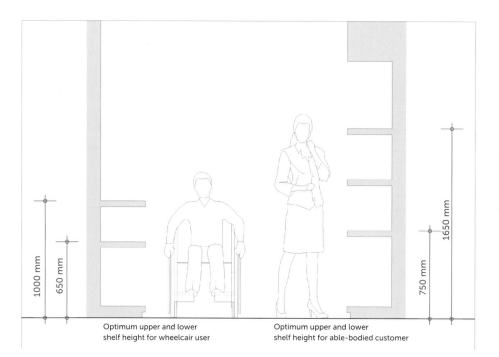

1000 mm

650 mm

Optimum upper and lower shelf height for wheelcair user

750 mm

1650 mm

Optimum upper and lower shelf height for able-bodied customer

Zones of optimum reach for wheelchair-bound and able-bodied customers.

touching product; at worse, where a customer has limited movement, shelves may be entirely outside their reach if placed too high or low. The optimum shelf heights for both able-bodied customers and those with restricted movement should be considered as the prime location for display. Where products are displayed outside these zones, the retailer must expect to offer assistance to customers to safely reach these locations.

Fitting Rooms

Store designers must recognize the needs of wheel-chair users, who should be provided with fitting rooms large enough to manoeuvre a wheelchair when trying on garments.

Able-bodied fitting rooms should be at least as large as shown in the diagram here and might be fitted

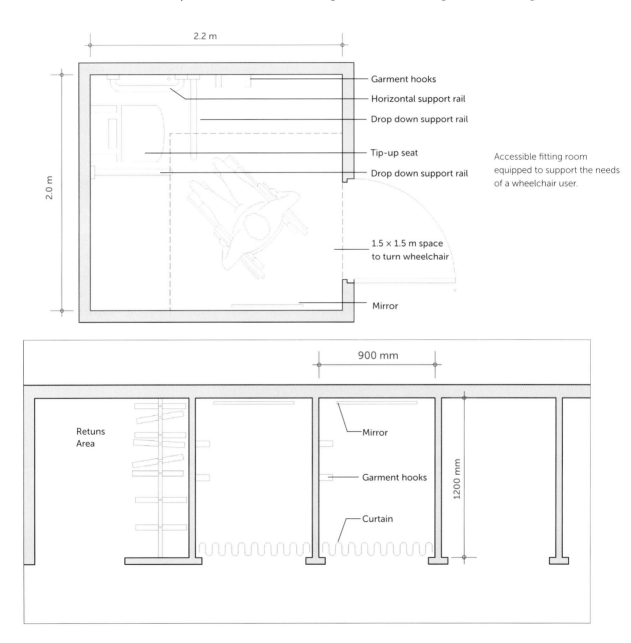

Accessible fitting room equipped to support the needs of a wheelchair user.

Typical fitting room block with garment return area.

with a full door for greater privacy or a curtain; in more relaxed environments a saloon-style half-door may be acceptable. In a busy store, good fitting-room management is dependent on a returns area from where discarded garments can be checked and returned to the sales floor.

Other considerations in the planning of fitting rooms are the locations of mirrors, whether these are to be communal or if the fitting room is sufficiently large enough to accommodate an individual mirror.

OTHER SPACE PLANNING REQUIREMENTS

Product Range

The product range determines the type of display furniture that will be required in the store, whether this involves garments that require hanging rails, precious watches that require secure vitrines or product that requires simple shelving. Not only must the range of merchandise be understood but also how the product range is sold in separate groups, the most obvious division being by gender or age.

Assortment

Assortment decisions are numerous and will vary during the life of the store. The factors to consider are assortment width, line length and line consistency. Width refers to how many products will be offered in the store; length refers to the number of stock-keeping units (SKUs) in a given line; and consistency is how closely the SKUs are related. Where the store's assortment includes products from external brands, the assortment consideration should also address the ratio of branded to own-bought merchandise.

Capacity

Capacity is simply a measure of how much product can be stored, displayed and sold through the store. An understanding of a store's capacity is based on a variety of factors including the ratio of back of house stockroom to front of house display. The assessment of stockroom size is covered elsewhere in this book. It is also based on the business's ability to replenish stock, which, if this is frequent, might reduce the necessity to hold product in stock in the store. Each

The importance of line consistency recognized at Abercrombie & Fitch, Eston Town Center, Ohio.

Deploying very low density to reflect a higher price point. Forty Five Ten, Hudson Yards, New York.

piece of merchandise on display occupies physical space, and hanging rails and shelves can be designed to best fit the various shapes and size requirements. The display requirements do not end here though, as product density within the store must be considered. Historically, product density has been seen as an indicator of a brand's place in the market, with low density of display characteristic of the luxury market and high-density display associated with low-cost stores. This approach is flexible and even high-end stores will push greater densities at certain times such as seasonal sales.

Seasonal and Future Variations

What variation of merchandise will the store be expected to retail? Whilst the seasonal changes between heavier winter attire and lighter summer clothing are fairly obvious, how can the store design respond to long-term changes in product lines? The speed of change encountered in much of today's retail sector probably demands that stores become more flexible and more easily adaptable to the changes in product range.

Operational Requirements

Having gained an understanding of the site size, the capacity requirements and internal organization of the product offers, the designer must not neglect to consider how the store will function. The design brief will therefore set out the requirements for point of sale or tills, fitting rooms, staff welfare facilities and all other operational functions. These should be checked against any statutory regulations that apply.

Budget and Programme

The overall capital expenditure budget may be established from the outset, or the designer may be asked to work within square metre rates. As well as the designer being made aware of the budget numbers, it is important that a clear understanding is reached on what items are included or excluded from the budget. For example, are visual merchandising tools and mannequins expected to be included in the store designer's budget?

Women's Shoe Galleries at Selfridges, London. (Photo: Olivier Hess)

Chapter Three

Shaping the Interior

BEFORE LOOKING AT THE INTERIOR FINISHES of the store, it is worth considering how the internal spaces are formed to create a 'white box'.

White Box, Grey Box

Retailers and their designers often use these terms to refer to the state of a construction site at particular times. The most commonly heard term is 'white box': this is, as the term suggests, a site which has been stripped out and reconstructed as an interior shell. From this point, the retailer's finishes, furniture and product could be installed into the white box and the store could begin trading. In reality, the steps from white box to finished store may not be as straightforward, not least because the understanding of what constitutes a white box finish varies across the industry. For example, a department store or mall landlord may wish to retain responsibility for the floor material and its installation, whereas in other situations the white box definition may be the one most commonly understood as the interior shell with no finishes. The 'grey box' is an even less-developed site, nevertheless stripped out, possibly with utilities provided to the site into which the brand can connect their own services. A new grey box site is unlikely to include a storefront and as well as the interior partitions and linings, the incoming contractor may have to install their own floor screed or raised floor as part of the brand's fit-out works.

Grey box interior at time of handover to the fit-out contractor.

White box interior starting to take shape. (Photo: Hyphen)

TACKLING THE BOX

Wall Linings

It is very common in retail design to line or face the existing perimeter walls, and not to apply finishes to the existing wall surface. Of course, there will be instances where it is desirable to retain the grey box perimeter walls, for example original brickwork with a lot of character, or when the building is protected because it is historically significant. In these cases, the design may have to adapt to suit, but generally a new wall lining is created. A new lining offers several advantages. Firstly, it allows a more precise control over the internal dimensions of the store, ensuring not only that perimeter walls run true and flat, but

that they are constructed perpendicular to internal partitions. It is surprising how often seemingly square walls are found to be out of alignment by a couple of degrees once an accurate survey has been taken. Lining the wall offers further advantages in that the lining can be designed to support the perimeter display furniture, and the void between the lining and the original wall can be used to run concealed cables, for example for fixture lighting. In addition, a new lining ensures the best possible substrate for proposed finishes.

These details illustrate two methods used to form wall linings, although in practice a combination of these methods may be necessary to achieve the desired results. Channels fixed directly to a masonry wall can be adjusted with shims or packing to ensure

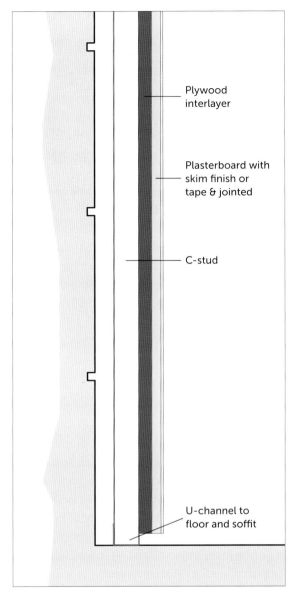

Plywood
interlayer

Plasterboard with
skim finish or
tape & jointed

C-stud

U-channel to
floor and soffit

**Wall lining using
studwork**

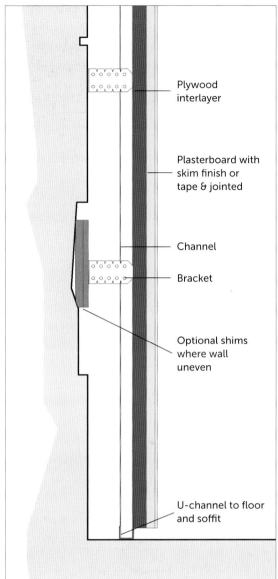

Plywood
interlayer

Plasterboard with
skim finish or
tape & jointed

Channel

Bracket

Optional shims
where wall
uneven

U-channel to floor
and soffit

**Wall lining using
channel system**

Wall lining details using dry-lining techniques.

that the finished wall runs true. Alternatively, a single-sided metal stud wall can be constructed directly in front of the perimeter, perhaps with ties to the original wall to ensure that it is adequately braced. Whilst it can be sufficient to line the wall only with plasterboard, a far more robust detail is to place a plywood interlayer under the plasterboard, with joints between sheets overlapped by the plasterboard. Not only does this create a far more rigid wall lining, but the plywood provides a robust substrate on which to mount fixtures or wall finishes. Usually the additional cost of installing a plywood interlayer is offset by the savings in not having to coordinate and fix battens and pattresses that would otherwise be required to bear the weight of wall-mounted fixtures. The plywood interlayer can also substitute for a second layer of plasterboard, which is often required to provide rigidity for wall finishes such as decorative plaster or wall tiling.

Plasterboard and Plastering

Plasterboard is a rigid sheet material formed of gypsum, sandwiched between two outer layers of lining paper and available in various thicknesses, the most commonly used being 9.5, 12.5 and 15 mm. Additives can be used to create boards with improved fire resistance or moisture resistance. Plasterboard can be easily cut on site and is secured onto a frame, usually of thin galvanized steel or softwood, using self-tapping screws. The major plasterboard manufacturers offer a range of framing and boarding components that allow linings and walls to be constructed easily to a given standard of strength, stability, acoustic and fire resistance. Unless the plasterboard is to be clad with another finishing material it is usually plastered using a variety of techniques, as described below.

Two-Coat Plaster

An undercoat of plaster of around 8mm thickness is applied but this thickness can be built up with further applications of plaster if necessary. Thinner finishing coats of around 2mm are then applied to obtain a smooth, flat finish.

Skim Plaster

Because skim plaster is essentially just a finish coat, the underlying surface must have been prepared to a reasonable degree of flatness. The plaster is usually applied in two coats: a 1mm undercoat followed by a 2mm topcoat applied before the undercoat dries.

Tape and Joint

The advantages of tape and jointing are that is does not require the same level of skill demanded by traditional plastering and it is quick to dry. The disadvantage is that the finishing process creates plaster dust which can be detrimental to other finishing trades, and so tape and joint finishing must be carefully managed in the construction programme. Tape and jointing is achieved through the application of a fibreglass tape over joints in the plasterboard, which is then filled over and made smooth. Where the adjacent plasterboard sheets are supplied with feathered edges, the joint is finished flush with the main boards. However, where cut boards or square edges occur, the joint will inevitably rise slightly above the surface of the plasterboard. Tape and jointing should not therefore be used in situations where an absolutely flat surface is demanded.

Ceilings

Look above your head in most retail stores and you will see that the ceiling, whether open or closed, is doing a lot to contribute to the character, ambience and functioning of the store. In most cases, it is the ceiling zone that carries the majority of the store's lighting, its mechanical and fire safety systems as well as the distribution network for electricity, communications and audio-visual equipment. The design of the ceiling contributes as much to a successful design as any other area. As well as providing the zone for these various services, the ceiling design affects the store's acoustics, acts as a mounting surface for hung fixtures and contributes to the overall ambience of the store. Retailers appreciate the quality of space that high ceilings help to create and the ceiling zone is always where designers look to rob the service engineer of workspace. Because of the ceiling's many functions, most ceiling finishes are formed from plasterboard which can be easily adapted to create flat ceilings, bulkheads, troughs and other features.

Ceiling framework installation. (Photo: Hyphen)

Finished ceiling with trough lighting, ventilation slots and other ceiling devices. (Photo: Hyphen)

Plasterboard ceilings are mounted on a grid of galvanized steel battens, which in turn is hung from the soffit on adjustable hanging rods. Care must be taken to coordinate the hanging of ductwork, conduit, cable trays and other building services components with the structure of the ceiling itself. Bulkheads, upstands and troughs can be formed from a combination of channels and battens, occasionally with plywood or MDF reinforcement. Ceiling troughs and rafts are widely used by designers as a means to conceal lighting, to make air-supply grilles less obtrusive or to have both functions located within the same trough.

Ceiling Trough Details

There are a number of recurring ceiling details that the designer will encounter. These arise through the need to create recesses or troughs for lighting or to conceal ventilation grilles. Most are formed through the combination of metal channel and plasterboard although proprietary systems are available, allowing for much cleaner and sharper trough edges.

Flooring Substrates

In most commercial environments, a reinforced concrete floor slab is likely to form part of the grey box specification. Exceptions to this might be older buildings and particularly on the upper floors of these buildings. The concrete floor slab is likely to be set well below the desired finished floor level and a sand-cement screed is usually laid over the slab to accommodate the difference in level and to provide a suitable substrate for the floor finishes. Where electrical or data connections are required to be made to mid-floor fixtures, conduits are run over the slab prior to the laying of the screed. Cables can then be drawn through the conduits for termination in a floor box or in the furniture piece itself. Whilst at first sight the pouring of a screed involves simply pouring to a depth that allows the installation of the floor finish, care must be given to the coordination of termination points so that furniture pieces are accurately located in the finished scheme. The choice of screed is also critical.

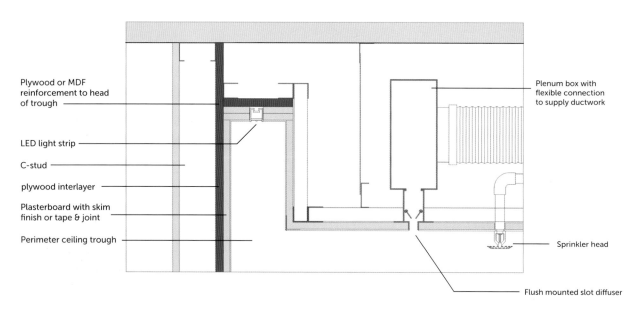

Plywood or MDF reinforcement to head of trough

LED light strip

C-stud

plywood interlayer

Plasterboard with skim finish or tape & joint

Perimeter ceiling trough

Plenum box with flexible connection to supply ductwork

Sprinkler head

Flush mounted slot diffuser

Light trough and air-supply diffusing detail.

Bonded Sand and Cement Screed

In this case, the screed is laid directly on a suitably prepared slab with the screed bonding, or adhering, to the substrate material. Bonded screeds can usually only be laid to a depth of 25–40mm as this lessens the risk of failure of the bond between substrate and screed.

Unbonded Sand and Cement Screed

Unbonded screeds are laid over a separating polythene membrane and to a minimum thickness of 70mm. When the difference between the substrate level and the finished floor level is substantial, an unbonded screed can be laid over expanded polystyrene which allows the level difference to be reduced without adding substantial additional mass.

Calcium Sulphate Self-Smoothing Screeds

These proprietary screeds are supplied pre-mixed and can be pumped directly to the location where they are to be laid, allowing much greater areas to be finished far more quickly than when applying a comparable sand and cement screed. Calcium sulphate screeds can be laid in either bonded and unbonded applications.

Vertical faces of a marble stone quarry.
(Photo: Azzollini Nicola Marmi)

Chapter Four

Materials and Finishes

THE VARIETY OF MATERIALS AVAILABLE TO the store designer is vast but they must be chosen with care. Consideration must be given to the cost of the material and its availability, as well as the workmanship required to successfully work or apply them. Some apparently simple materials such as decorative plaster require great skill to use effectively. As well as understanding the cost of materials and labour, the designer should also be aware of the longevity of the finishes selected, their maintenance cost and how they might be recycled or repurposed in the future. Rather than grouping materials by their type alone, this chapter considers the area of application and the options available to the specifier.

FLOOR FINISHES

The floor is the most used and abused surface of the store, subject to heavy foot traffic and the tracking of trolleys and pallet trucks. Retail floors are always vulnerable to damage caused by the dirt and grime carried in on shoes from the street. It is therefore vital that the floor material be selected with wear and ease of cleaning in mind. Most typically, the ideal retail floor is a hard surface that meets the above criteria, but not always so. Some retail environments, such as those selling high-end fashion and jewellery, may demand the luxurious ambience offered by a carpeted floor. Some watch retailers may even insist on a carpeted floor as an insurance against breakages from careless handling of their stock. Shoe retailers may demand both a hard and soft floor finish: a carpet is nicer to walk on barefoot between trying on shoes, whereas a harder surface is needed to truly test a shoe for comfort and fit.

No floor should be hazardous to walk over but this cannot always be guaranteed if the flooring material becomes wet. The risk of this will vary from high-risk situations where the store trades at street level where rain can easily make the first few metres of floor wet, to low-risk upper floors of department stores or the innermost units of shopping malls. Regardless of the application or location, there are standards and codes to be observed and these may state the maximum levels of slipperiness that are acceptable in any given location. No flooring material should be specified without establishing these criteria and understanding the environment into which it is being installed.

Slip Resistance

When specifying the flooring material, and in particular stone, ceramic or porcelain tile, it is important to understand the slip resistance of the material so that it can be checked for suitability. A requirement to protect people against slipping exists in different jurisdictions around the world, and in the UK it is the Workplace (Health, Safety and Welfare) Regulations that impose this requirement. The UK's Health and Safety Executive assesses a material's resistance to slip using a pendulum test based on an imitation shoe heel, swung over the surface of the test material. The resulting pendulum test value (PTV) can be used to describe the degree of slip resistance but the test conditions should imitate the environment into which it is installed, as results will vary if the

Slip Resistance

PTV	DIN R-value for shod feet	Non-slip properties
11–18	R9	Very poor
18–34	R10	Poor
34–51	R11	Unsuitable in most commercial applications
51–70	R12	Minimum recommended standard
70 and above	R13	Best slip resistance

Comparison between the PTV and the DIN standard of slip resistance.

material is wet or contaminated with oil or grease.

Many European manufacturers and suppliers state slip resistance for their products based on the *Deutsche Industrie Norm* (DIN) method from Germany. This testing method aims to assess slipperiness by testing across a range of conditions, from bare feet covered with a soap solution to cleated safety boots with oil as a contaminate. Testing is carried out on a variety of ramp gradients to establish slipping points and the results given as a grade, stated as an R number to represent *Rutschfesigkeit* or slip resistance. Assessing if a material's slip resistance is adequate for the proposed use is therefore dependent on understanding the environment into which it is installed, the type of sole likely to be in contact with the surface and the likelihood of water or contaminates being present. Where these variables are likely to result in unusual outcomes, the designer must seek material certification as proof of a material's properties and verify the required standard with the appropriate statutory authority.

Natural Stone

The principal natural stone types can be sourced from quarries around the world and generally delivered to the stone cutting mill in blocks of around 6–8m³ in size. When intended for use as a sheet material, the block is cut into slabs of the required thickness, typically 20–40mm, but this can be determined by the character and physical properties of the stone. The stone slabs are then cut to the required size, and shaped and polished or honed to the required finish. When specifying stone flooring, the designer is faced with a wide choice of stone types, colours and patterns. What must not be overlooked, however, is that because stone is a natural material, differences in colour and pattern can occur and these variations can manifest themselves even in blocks cut from the same quarry. For large projects which are likely to be completed over time and in phases it is important to manage the procurement of the stone to ensure that stone is delivered to match a common control sample. Where natural variations can be predicted to occur, stone tiles cut from a variety of blocks should be mixed to ensure that no single or unusual pattern dominates a given area of the floor. Where stone patterns are very distinctive, the tiles should ideally be dry-laid for the designer's approval before being fixed permanently.

The research body, The Ornamental Stone Network, estimates that around 2,500 unique ornamental stone types can be found in Europe alone, with the most significant quarries located in Mediterranean Europe. Over the last twenty years, the European market has also seen a significant influx of stone from quarries located in China, India, Turkey and Latin America and, in particular, Brazil. From the vast range of natural stones available to the designer, there are a number that are most usually encountered.

Basalt

This is a hard volcanic stone with excellent durability, available in varying grey shades through to black and with a fairly monolithic or consistent pattern.

Granite

A hard igneous rock with a coarse-grained crystalline appearance, this stone generally has a consistency of pattern with little or no veining and can be found in a wide variety of colours, including black, white, blue and red.

Limestone

A sedimentary rock that was formed from the skeletal remains of marine organisms, limestone is relatively soft and easily worked and has been used as a building material for thousands of years. It is

Granite colours and patterns. L to R: Porpora, Labrador and Kashmir. (Photo: Azzollini Nicola Marmi)

Albaperla limestone slabs. (Photo: Azzollini Nicola Marmi)

Arabescato marble slabs cut and book-matched. (Photo: Azzollini Nicola Marmi)

porous and surface sealing may be required if it is to be used in a retail interior. The appearance of the stone is generally monolithic and the colour typically cream to grey, although blue and black limestone is also available.

Marble

A metamorphic rock, marble is easily worked and was traditionally the stone of choice for sculpting and decorative work. The beauty of marble lies in its veining, caused by impurities in the limestone from which it was formed when it was subjected to intense heat and pressure. Well-known varieties include the white Carrara with grey veins, Breccia which has warm pink tones and Calacatta with its darker veining. Black marble is also available, with varying degrees of white or grey veining.

Quartzite

A hard metamorphic rock, almost entirely formed of quartz, this can be found in a spectrum of colours, from white to dark grey and many neutral tones. The stone pattern can range from fairly plain to veined.

Slate

This is a sedimentary rock, which can be readily split to make thin tiles or sawn into thicker slabs. Slate is available in many shades of grey as well as blue, green and purple; it characteristically has a monolithic texture with only light veining.

Stone Sizing

Natural stone tiles can be cut to any shape or size, subject to the physical constraints of the original material. Where large-format tiles are required (that is to say, a stone tile greater than around 600mm square), the specifier should appreciate the cost implications. Firstly, the larger the tile, the greater the amount of waste material resulting from the cut slab. The efficiencies of cutting many tiles, say 200mm or 300mm square, from a slab are self-evident, meaning that the smaller format is generally a more economic option. The next consideration is the transport and manual handling, which becomes more difficult with large-format tiles and increases the risk of breakage in transit. The final consideration is the waste factor on site. A small-format tile might be laid with a narrow margin of waste of 5–10 per cent to allow for cut tiles and rejected material, whereas the waste from larger formats is proportionally greater and so an allowance of 10–15 per cent or more might be required.

All natural stone is porous, but it can be made more resistant to staining through polishing. Polishing is usually carried out in the stone mill to one side of the slab only. Whilst highly polished stone can give an impressive finish, care must be taken where there is any risk of the floor becoming wet so as to avoid the surface becoming a slip hazard. A honed or matt finish can improve the slip resistance of the surface as can other surface finishes such as sand-blasted, riven, bush-hammered, flamed and ruled. Natural stone floors that have been laid and found not to offer enough slip resistance can be treated with an acid-based chemical treatment to lightly etch the surface.

Trompe l'oeil stone pattern at Gucci, Copenhagen Airport. (Photo: Hyphen)

Lapis grey marble flooring, honed to ensure a suitable public area finish, at Hudson Yards, New York.

Because natural stone is rigid, it requires that the substructure onto which it is to be laid should be both stable and able to support the imposed load. Consider, for example, replacing a traditional oak floor with a thickness of 19mm in order to lay 20mm marble floor tiles: the load on the floor increases by a factor of three and a half to 0.54 kN/m². The cost of any strengthening and additional work to the floor substrate must be considered in any cost calculations when pricing stonework. Natural stone tiles must be firmly bedded, usually on a cement-based adhesive to a thickness of between 1mm and 15mm. Where the stone is naturally porous, care must be taken not to use an adhesive that will leach water through the slab to stain the top surface; a rapid-drying adhesive can sometimes overcome this problem. For a very clean-looking floor finish, the joint width between tiles need only be 1mm but sometimes wider joints are used for aesthetic reasons, for instance to show off tumbled stone to best effect. Grouts used to finish the job are available in a wide variety of colours to either complement or contrast with the stone colour.

Terrazzo

When discussing stone floor finishes, terrazzo should also be included. The technique for laying terrazzo is described by Italian scholar Francesco Sansovino in the sixteenth century but this is probably derived from earlier Roman mosaic methods. Traditionally the terrazzo is laid *in situ* with marble stone chips placed in a lime cement. A similar technique called *seminato* uses much smaller stone chips to give a denser, closer-grained finish. Once the floor has hardened it is ground smooth and polished. Terrazzo can be very long-lasting but can be prone to cracking and so is best laid in fields, which are bound by metal edge profiles to allow expansion to take place without affecting the integrity of the terrazzo. The range of colours can be controlled through the selection of the marble aggregate and so choice is wide, although typically the floor is white to grey with colour accents.

Two options are available to the designer when working with terrazzo: traditional *in situ* casting and precast panels or tiles. Laying the terrazzo *in situ* can be time-consuming but if the method can be accommodated the result is a monolithic floor without the usual tile joints. Skirtings, nosings and other edge details can be formed as part of the same process, giving terrazzo its unique flowing character.

Precast terrazzo panels are available in a greater range of sizes than traditional stone, the limits being the size of the production mould and the subsequent handling. Sheets for floor and wall applications are typically produced in thicknesses of between 10mm and 20mm and applied using similar techniques to stonework.

Marmoreal precast terrazzo tile at Forty Five Ten, Hudson Yards, New York.

Circular stone tiles cast in terrazzo at Väla Centrum, Helsingborg, Sweden.

Ceramic and Porcelain Tile

Tiling provides a durable, easily laid and economic floor finish in a wide variety of colours and patterns. Ceramic tiles are made from fired clay whilst silica and feldspar are added to the clay to make porcelain tiles. Porcelain tiles are fired at higher temperatures and the resulting tile is harder and denser than a ceramic tile. The density of porcelain tiles make them less absorbent than ceramic tiles. Ceramic tiles, on the other hand, are generally cheaper and easier to cut.

Ceramic and porcelain tiles can be supplied unglazed or glazed, the glazing comprising a surface coating of liquid glass which is applied during the firing stage. The glazing protects the body of the tile and can be finished matt or gloss, which in turn can affect the slip rating of the tile. Because unglazed tiles do not rely on this surface treatment, the tile colour runs through the body of the tile, so a chip in the surface will not show as a different colour. Unglazed tiles offer a utilitarian, earthy colour pallet, whilst glazed tiles offer an infinite variety of colour and pattern.

Traditional stone mosaic flooring detail at the Victoria Quarter, Leeds, West Yorkshire.

Hard-wearing porcelain tiles finished to resemble timber flooring at Nespresso, Liverpool One. (Photo: Hyphen)

Resin Flooring

Epoxy resin is a relatively modern invention, first synthesized in the 1930s. Its use as a flooring material was not seen commercially until the 1980s and at the time it was principally used in manufacturing facilities and particularly where hygiene considerations were important, such as in food preparation. The seamless finish that is achievable and the industrial aesthetic that results has made resin flooring an increasingly popular choice for retail design. Multiple coats may be required to achieve the desired finish and the material is either flow-applied or trowelled and then cured through the application of a hardener. The colour, finish and slip resistance of resin flooring can be adjusted through the material specification to suit the project brief and patterns can be achieved by adding vinyl flakes during the installation.

Epoxy Resin

This is generally applied thinly by trowel or roller and is prone to wear. A good colour choice is available and epoxy resin is usually the least expensive option, although the cure time can be slow, which may affect other construction activity.

Polyurethane

This is a more robust material, with excellent resistance to cracking but costing more than epoxy resin. Due to its higher cost, polyurethane is probably best suited to high-traffic back of house areas, where epoxy resin might not offer sufficient resistance. Polyurethane is applied trowelled or poured to a self-smooth finish.

PMMA (Polymethyl Methacrylate Catalyst)

This finish is highly customable to achieve good anti-slip properties and resistance to chemical contamination. It is laid at a thickness of up to 9mm and for the retail designer it can be a useful finish in highly trafficked areas because of its rapid cure (hardening) time.

Before considering the application of a resin floor, the integrity of the substrate must be checked. The ideal subfloor is a concrete deck with little or minimal deflection (flex).

Epoxy resin mix using two colours to obtain a concrete effect at Zurheide in Düsseldorf.

Polished Concrete and Concrete Effect

Polished concrete is often bracketed alongside resin flooring because they share a similar industrial aesthetic although the two finishes are achieved quite differently. A hybrid of the two methods is also now widely used, known as micro concrete topping.

A true polished concrete floor finish is achieved by grinding and polishing hardened concrete using specialist tools. The finished floor that results will naturally reflect the aggregates present in the concrete. Where a new concrete floor is laid with the specific intention of polishing, the aggregate composition can be considered in advance. Chemical densifiers can also be added which act to fill holes and pores in the concrete, leading to fewer or no voids in the finished floor. The grinding is carried out using diamond tools with progressively finer cutting properties until the desired level of sheen has been achieved. The floor is then sealed with a penetrative sealant allowing the concrete to breathe. Polished concrete floors, whether created from an existing floor or a newly poured floor, usually work best when conveying a found or distressed aesthetic. Polished concrete floor finishes that are too precise or unblemished tend to lose their character.

Micro concrete finish around a field of parquet at Paul Smith, Coal Drops Yard, London.

Interior of Paul Smith, Coal Drops Yard, London.

Stainless steel branding inset in concrete threshold, Hudson Yards, New York.

Micro concrete is a cementitious material that is applied by trowel to a thickness of as little as 2–3 mm. Once set, the appearance is that of a smooth screed floor. The colour and finish can be adjusted in the material mix and concrete-like effects can be achieved, such as cloudiness or stain patterns. Because the application of the material is thin, a concrete appearance can be obtained even in situations where potential floor loads are limited. The great advantage of the material is that it can also be applied to vertical surfaces in situations where the finish required is the same for walls and floor.

Timber

Timber as a flooring material can be inexpensive and easily worked. In the retail environment, however, care must be taken to ensure that the timber floor specified is robust enough to withstand commercial foot traffic. A timber floor may require more regular maintenance to ensure that it continues to look good, as it can be easily damaged and marked. Timber floors should not be used where they may become wet as wood can easily warp and become misshapen.

Plank Flooring

Solid wood flooring is made from wooden planks, machined with tongue and groove edges that interlock to form a continuous floor. To prevent movement, the planks must be fixed, ether by secret nailing through the tongue or glued to the substrate using a proprietary adhesive. Secret nailing or screwing is used for timber or plywood substrates and adhesives used for solid substrates such as screed or concrete.

Because the planks are cut from natural wood, the sizes available vary according to the species of tree. Typically, planks are 15–20mm thick with a width between 90mm and 200mm. Unlike engineered planks, the lengths supplied tend to be random, usually between 300mm and 1200mm. More skill is required to lay a solid wood floor as the lengths need to be matched and adjusted to ensure that joints between strips do not coincide.

On the surface, an engineered floor may appear similar to a solid timber floor, but the planks have a different composition. An engineered floor comprises a plywood or high-density fibreboard core with a thin-layer hardwood finish to the top surface and a balancing veneer to the underside. The various layers

Narrow strip-faced planks provide a warm and smooth-flowing floor finish through the Emporia Mall in Malmö, Sweden.

Nicely worn herringbone pattern parquet at Jack Wills, Heathrow Airport Terminal 3, London.

can be laid so that their grain runs perpendicular to the top surface, resulting in a strong and very stable flooring material. The top surface varies in thickness from a thin veneer to a substantial layer of around 6mm, with plank thickness ranging from 10mm to 20mm. A thicker top surface allows the floor to be refurbished several times through sanding without exposing the inner core.

Engineered planks are generally of a fixed size and larger than those available in solid wood. Widths of over 200mm and plank lengths of over 2m are not uncommon. Typically, wider planks are composed of two or three narrower strips of top surface wood, giving the appearance of a narrower plank floor. Planks are supplied with tongue and grove edges and the stability offered by engineered planks also allows them to be supplied as click-system floors which can be laid to float over an existing floor, usually on a suitable underlay. A laminate floor is similar in principle to an engineered floor but the top surface is replaced with a high-pressure laminate. Because of its poor wearing properties and vulnerability to chipping, such a floor is unlikely to be suitable in the retail environment.

Parquet is a technique for laying floors by using small wooden blocks and it originated in seventeenth-century France. The traditional parquet block size is usually 280mm × 70 mm with a thickness of 15–18mm, although longer and wider variants can be found, as can square blocks that can be incorporated into the pattern and hexagonal blocks that form a honeycomb pattern. Like plank flooring, parquet can be sourced as a tongue and groove, solid or an engineered wood product. It is fixed using the same techniques as plank flooring although the Versailles pattern is usually too intricate to be laid *in situ* and so is generally supplied as a complete panel.

Parquet lends itself to a number of traditional patterns.

Hardwood species are generally used for timber floors due to their good wearing properties and resistance to foot traffic. Whilst timber floors are able to withstand reasonably heavy traffic, dents from stiletto heels and heavily loaded trolley wheels can occur and so the designer should anticipate a reasonable degree of wear and tear during the life of the floor whatever the species selected. Tropical hardwoods which were traditionally prized for their durability, particularly teak, wenge and mahogany, should now be avoided by the specifier due to concerns over deforestation and illegal logging. Wherever a hardwood is specified, the designer should verify that it is from a responsibly managed source recognized by the Forestry Stewardship Council.

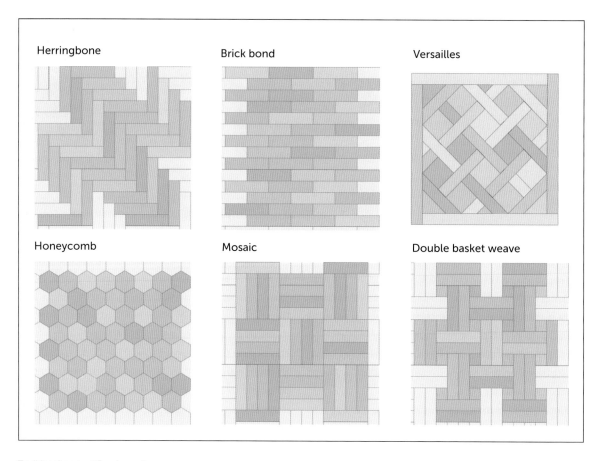

Traditional parquet flooring patterns.

Typical grain characteristics for commonly specified hardwoods. Top, L to R: oak, cherry, maple, walnut. Bottom, L to R: oak (smoked finish), bamboo, beech, ash.

Oak

This is a widely available flooring timber. When cut from heartwood, the pattern of oak is very uniform with little or no pattern or colour change and is used for premium grade products. Other grades might include planks with a greater number of knots or colour variations where the pattern cuts through the lighter sapwood.

Cherry

Cherry is a soft hardwood with less resistance to impact and more prone to darkening over time where exposed to sunlight. It is patterned with a tight wavy grain and with red and pink hues.

Walnut

This is a soft hardwood and so should be used with care in heavily trafficked areas. It does have very good colour stability where exposed to sunlight; colours range from rich purply-browns to cream.

Maple

This is a very hard wood with excellent durability. It is light in colour but takes on a warmer golden hue with age.

Beech

Beech is a soft hardwood, light in colour with reddish hues.

Ash

This is a soft hardwood, with light and creamy brown tones and bold grain pattern.

Bamboo

Bamboo is a perennial grass rather than a hardwood, but it can be manufactured into conventional tongue and groove boards through the gluing together of several narrow strips or by the shredding and compression of bamboo fibres into a plank. This technique

Original timber flooring retained at McQ, London. (Photo: Hyphen)

is known as strand woven and it produces a very durable material that can be used in a commercial environment. The colours range from golden brown to darker shades.

Timber Floor Finishes

Wooden floor components can be supplied pre-finished or in a natural state to be finished on site. Pre-finished treatments include ultraviolet lacquer, which comprises multiple coats of factory-applied lacquer which is cured under ultraviolet light. Where unfinished wood is laid, it will be necessary to finish the floor *in situ*. Prior to the finish coat, the floor may be sanded to achieve a more uniform surface or wire-brushed to accentuate the natural grain. The floor can also be stained to adjust the colour and then lacquered or oiled. A lacquered finish can range from gloss to matt and requires several coats to achieve a durable finish. Unlike an oiled finish,

if the lacquer is scratched or gouged, the raw wood is exposed.

Finishing oils are based on natural plant oils and waxes plus drying agents and water-repellents. The finish is flatter and less glossy than a lacquer and because the oil soaks into the grain of the wood, surface scratches are less noticeable. Because the floor must be oiled periodically to maintain its condition, an oiled floor should not be specified unless there is a well-organized maintenance regime in place after the store opens.

Sheet Materials

Linoleum

This traditional flooring material is made from linseed oil, resin, cork particles and calcium carbonate. It is supplied in both roll and tile form, with a thickness typically around 2–3.5mm, and it is available in a range of colours. Traditionally linoleum has a slightly

Oak plank flooring on the upper level walkways of Stockholm's Täby Mall contrasts with the limestone finish on the lower level.

marbled or cloudy appearance. The material is fixed by means of a suitable adhesive but care must be taken when working with rolls of linoleum as it remains brittle when cold. A cheaper PVC sheet material, developed in the 1930s, is now far more widely used.

Polyvinyl Chloride (PVC)

PVC is a synthetic plastic polymer and is used to manufacture what is commonly referred to as vinyl flooring. This is manufactured in 4mm-thickness sheets or tiles and in a wide variety of colours and finishes, including a slip-resistant surface. Vinyl is fixed to the flooring substrate using a proprietary adhesive and because of its excellent durability and impact resistance is most often specified for back of house areas. PVC joints can be welded and this detail is particularly helpful where PVC skirtings are required.

Carpets and Rugs

In busy retail applications, carpet is not often a suitable floor finish due to its vulnerability to damage caused by heavy foot traffic. However, for some situations such as private sales rooms, areas of the store offering a higher level of customer service, or where the product demands it, carpet is specified. In these situations, the designer will typically look to a woven carpet which offers a high-quality product and good scope for selecting colour, pile type, pile depth and yarn. Woven carpets are made by weaving a surface yarn into the backing material with the yarn then cut at the required length or left as a loop. The yarn is usually 100 per cent wool or a mix of 80 per cent wool and 20 per cent nylon. A woven carpet must be laid on an underlay pad of either polyurethane, synthetic rubber or felt. The carpet is fixed using a combination of tack strips and gluing, with joints between adjacent seams either sewn or sealed and glued. Where the carpeted floor lies adjacent to a hard surface, or forms an island in a hard floor, it should sit in a recessed well to ensure that its exposed edge is not a trip hazard.

Rugs can be manufactured from the same materials as a woven carpet as well as silk, cotton and many synthesized fibres. Rugs are a potential trip

Inset broadloom carpet at Alexander McQueen, Paris. (Photo: Hyphen)

Inset carpet creates a focal point for display furniture and relief from the adjacent hard surfaces. Lacoste, Westfield London. (Photo: Hyphen)

hazard and so would generally not be placed on heavily trafficked walkways. They can, however, be successfully used for decoration or to soften the character of a harder subfloor. When placing rugs into the retail environment they should be secured to prevent movement of the rug across the floor; this can be achieved with an anti-slip underlay sheet or double-sided adhesive tape.

Loose-laid rug emphasizes fixture location in Gucci, Perisur, Mexico City. (Photo: Hyphen)

Entrance Mats

Where the entrance to the store is directly from the street, it is worthwhile considering placing an entrance mat immediately inside the door. As it is generally reckoned to require six steps across an entrance mat for it to be fully effective, and as most stores do not have the space or the desire to fill their entrance threshold with such large mats, the mat should be specified to give the best result possible. The store designer should understand the likely levels of foot traffic so that the mat specification can be checked against the manufacturer's claimed standards. A lightly trafficked entrance might see fewer than eighty people per hour entering the store, whereas a heavily trafficked entrance could see upwards of 800 people per hour. Where the same entrance serves as an entrance for stock trolleys or pallet trucks, the mat's finish should allow for this additional occasional load. The choice of mat may also be governed by the available matwell depth, which can be dependent on the choice of floor finish.

Coir

The traditional entrance mat is coir or woven coconut fibre, and this is still used primarily for its aesthetic appeal and ease of application. Coir matting can be supplied by the roll and so can be cut to unusual shapes. The coir material is mounted on a PVC backing and is usually loose laid in a matwell of the appropriate depth. The thickness of the mat is typically 14–24mm, but the height can usually be finessed if a plywood base is included in the matwell design to allow a degree of height adjustment. Coir matting can be supplied in its natural light brown colour or can be dyed, usually grey or black, and logos can be over-printed. Coir is effective at removing dust and absorbing some foot-trafficked rainwater, but it is unsuitable in areas that are likely to often get wet because water is slow to wick away from the coir fibres. In applications where the traffic is very heavy, the designer should recognize that stained and worn coir is likely to have to be replaced as part of the store's annual maintenance programme. When specifying the thickness of coir matting, the designer should recognize that thicker mats may not be ideal for wheelchair traffic because they compress, or 'give', under load.

Synthetic Woven Fabrics

Like coir, woven fabrics of synthetic nylon such as polypropylene can usually be supplied and cut to suit any required shape or size. Alternatively, polypropylene fabric matting can be supplied as carpet tiles with a rubber backing to be glued in place. The range of colours available is usually extensive, and the thickness of the mat is thin, usually between 7mm and 12mm, including ribbing to improve dirt trapping. In situations where it is not possible to create a deep enough matwell, a polypropylene mat may offer a solution.

Hybrid Mats

Hybrid mats are generally comprised of linked aluminium or PVC profiles that carry a variety of surface finishes such as aluminium scraper bars, nylon brushes and polypropylene woven fibre strips. The variety of colours and materials is wide and graphics or logos can be incorporated if required. The depth of the mat varies according to the specification and the manufacturer, but between 12mm and 24mm should generally be allowed. The mat is rigid, giving a problem-free surface for wheelchairs and delivery trolleys. Hybrid mats can be made to either a closed or an open construction. An open mat allows the dirt that collects on the scrapers and brushes to fall between the profiles to collect in the bottom of the matwell; the mat is then rolled back to allow this debris to be cleared away. A closed construction must be surface-cleaned like a more traditional mat.

Decorative synthetic woven fabric entrance mat at 10 Corso Como, New York.

Hybrid entrance mat.

Matwells

For aesthetic reasons, and to avoid potential trip hazards, the entrance mat should always be set flush with the surrounding floor finish. This is achieved by creating a matwell to the required depth, framing the well's lip with a metal profile that is set into the main floor finish as it is laid.

WALLS AND CEILINGS FINISHES

There is a large overlap between the finishes used to decorate internal walls and those used on the ceiling and so it makes sense to consider these jointly. Paint finishes can be applied to both surfaces just as stone can also be mounted to both, although the technical challenges of fixing stone to a ceiling or soffit are not to be underestimated.

Staircase Treads

Where the store design includes a staircase, the designer will be faced with a decision on whether the main floor finishes can also be used on the stair treads. Consideration needs to be given to the suitability of the material. For example, a new steel staircase is likely to deflect (flex) more than a solid floor and so tiles or terrazzo that are prone to cracking might prove unsuitable. Where stone tiling is used as the main floor finish, it may be worth considering having thicker stair treads cut from the same stone to reduce or eliminate tile joints. To avoid trips and falls, building regulations require that the edge of the stair tread can be visually identified, usually with a contrasting colour. Depending on the material being used, a number of solutions are possible to ensure that this requirement is met without compromising the character of the flooring material. These include inlaid metal strips or stair nosings of contrasting colour and texture.

Stone

Care must be taken in the use of stone as a wall finish because whilst small-format wall tiles can be adhered to a suitable substrate, large panels must be mechanically fixed. Where the substrate is a masonry or concrete wall of sufficient strength, the stone panels can be supported on stainless steel anchors attached to the wall. Alternatively, a steel frame can be constructed on which the stone panels can be hung. An understanding of the thickness of the stone cladding is critical to successful design. Thin stone tiles can be fixed using adhesive, but larger, heavier panels must be secured with anchors. Where the panel is mechanically fixed, a minimum thickness for the stone must be allowed: this is to stop the stone spalling or fracturing around the anchor fixings. Generally, most stone types require a minimum panel thickness of 20mm but for limestones this increases to 50mm. Clearly,

the mass of 50mm-thick limestone panels requires a considerable degree of structural support which has given rise to the technique of applying stone veneers to a much lighter substrate, usually to an aluminium honeycomb substrate.

Backlit Onyx

Onyx and marble are closely related, with onyx's characteristic translucency and wide variety of colours and patterns making it a desirable wall finish. Onyx lends itself to being backlit and can be cut as thin as 6mm when bonded to a polycarbonate substrate. Large slabs of highly patterned decorative stone can be particularly effective when book-matched: in this case two consecutive slabs cut from the same block are polished on opposite surfaces so that a mirror effect is achieved when the two are mounted side by side.

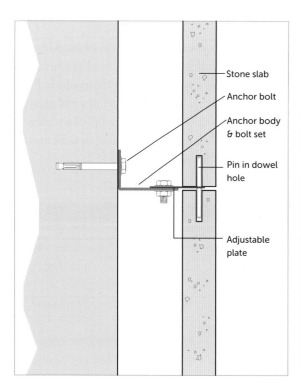

Stone slab
Anchor bolt
Anchor body & bolt set
Pin in dowel hole
Adjustable plate

Stone slab anchor system

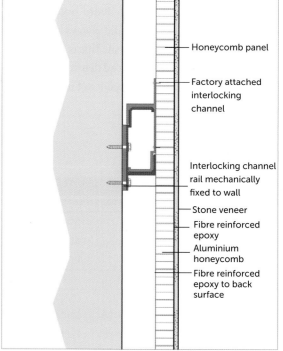

Honeycomb panel
Factory attached interlocking channel
Interlocking channel rail mechanically fixed to wall
Stone veneer
Fibre reinforced epoxy
Aluminium honeycomb
Fibre reinforced epoxy to back surface

Honeycomb stone veneer panel fixing

Fixing methods for stone slabs and aluminium honeycomb-backed stone veneers.

Stone Veneers

As noted above, the structural engineering work to safely support the mass of traditional stone panels can mean that this material is not viable in a project. In these instances, using stone as a veneer is a possible alternative. A stone veneer, usually of 6mm thickness, is bonded to an aluminium backing of honeycomb cellular construction, typically 12–24mm thick. Whilst considerably more expensive than a traditional stone slab, the big advantage is that the weight of a typical panel is only one third of the solid equivalent. Where the edge of the honeycomb sheet is visible, for example on the outer corner of a stone-faced wall, the edge must be lipped by means of a mitre-jointed edge strip.

Decorative Plasters

This group of finishes includes polished plaster in a variety of colours and surface finishes and using traditional materials and application techniques dating back at least to Roman times. The character of polished plaster is achieved using marble which is ground to a dust and mixed with slaked lime and cement. The finish is usually achieved through the initial application of a key coat, followed by multiple layers of the finishing coat worked in small areas and to the desired texture. The surface can be finished smooth or textured, pitted or riven to resemble the surface of natural stone. Once the plaster has dried out, wax can be applied to protect and enhance the finish. Venetian plaster is a sub-group of polished plaster made from lime putty and marble dust which is burnished to give a highly polished finish resembling marble stonework. Polished plaster is often used to give a joint-free monolithic wall finish with a strong depth of character but the store designer should understand that there are particular constraints in the use of polished plaster. From a construction point of view, polished plaster should only be applied to a stable substrate as it is vulnerable to movement cracks. The worktime and drying times are quite long and a high standard of finish can only be achieved in a clean, dust-free environment. For these reasons, polished plaster work must be programmed carefully into the construction sequence. Whilst polished plaster is reasonably robust, if damage occurs it may prove difficult to patch-repair to the same finish as the original work. Polished plaster should therefore be avoided in areas where it is likely to be subjected to knocks and scrapes.

Honeycomb stone sample. (Photo: Azzollini Nicola Marmi)

Paint and Colour Referencing

The successful selection of paint colours can become problematic, particularly where the designer bases their colour palette on a manufacturer's range that is not easily available commercially to the contractor, and then only at high cost. Colour comparison websites such as e-paint.co.uk can be used to find the closest match between different paint ranges, but often the results are only approximations. Where a sample of the desired colour is available, it can be scanned and paint mixed to match. In all cases, sample areas should be prepared so that options can be compared and the final result approved. The majority of paint reference systems are interchangeable between manufacturers, with NCS and RAL widely available across Europe.

Natural Colour System (NCS)

The NCS was developed in Sweden in the 1970s and is founded on visual assessments of colour perception. The colour reference is generally in two parts comprising the nuance and the hue, with each component a precise location in a three-dimensional colour space. Whilst the NCS reference system could potentially identify ten million colours, the standard range, prefixed with 'S', today comprises 1,950 colours.

Reichs-Ausschuß für Lieferbedingungen (RAL)

RAL originated in Germany in 1927 as a collection of forty colours identified by a numeric reference and intended to establish a common standard across industry. Whilst NCS is based on colour theory, the origins of RAL are in paint specification and by the 1960s the RAL Classic range had grown to 210 colours for matt finishes with a slightly smaller subset for a gloss finish. RAL Classic references are four digits, with RAL 9010 universally known amongst store designers and fit-out contractors as pure white. RAL Design was launched in 1993 and currently offers a far wider palette of 1,825 colours with no overlap of the Classic range. RAL Design references comprise seven digits which locate the colour in the CIELAB colour space, a system developed by the International Commission on Illumination in the 1970s.

British Standard (BS 4800)

In a similar way to the RAL Classic colours, the BS 4800 range is designed as a standard collection for building purposes which have been selected from the wider spectrum of BS 5252. The system was developed in the early 1970s with the aim of establishing an economic range of eighty-eight colours that could be specified with confidence, particularly on public building projects. As of 2016, the range stands at

Colour swatches and paint manufacturers' colour cards.

122 colours to reflect the demands of the market. Colours are allocated a three-part code, referencing hue, greyness and weight.

Pantone

The Pantone Matching System (PMS) is a system developed in the US in the 1950s by Pantone LLC. Its origins lie in the print business and today is widely used by graphic designers and printers to ensure consistency of colour when designs are put into production. Pantone publishes a range of 1,867 PMS colours, described with a three- or four-digit code; for example PMS 1837, which is the robin's-egg blue trademarked to Tiffany. Designers working exclusively from the PMS palette may encounter difficulties in finding

Farrow & Ball showroom, Paris. (Photo: Hyphen)

paint colours that precisely match the ink colours from which Pantone's system is derived.

Manufacturers' Own Reference Systems

NCS, RAL and BS colours are standards against which paint is manufactured by several manufacturers. However, many companies offer paints using their own reference system, or simply by name, which is common in the domestic market. These paint collections tend to change more frequently as home decoration fashions move on and so the consistency of a standard reference system is not required. The UK company Farrow & Ball offers around 130 paint colours at any given time, with older colours archived as newer ones enter their range. The colours carry evocative names and a simple reference, such as Setting Plaster, No. 231. In the US, Benjamin Moore offers 1,680 Classic range colours which are described using a similar referencing method.

The ICI Paints colour palette notation system is a proprietary system, developed in the UK by Imperial Chemical Industries, acquired by Dutch company AkzoNobel in 2008. ICI Paint's brand Dulux is widely available in both the trade and domestic markets, offering around 1,200 standard colours. The ICI notation system is a three-part reference comprising hue, light refractive value and chroma.

Polychromatic paint finish at Paul Smith, Coal Drops Yard, London.

Traditional storefront in Bakewell, Derbyshire.

Chapter Five

Storefronts

A POTENTIAL CUSTOMER'S FIRST IMPRESSION of the store is likely to be the storefront and the immediate retail space that lies beyond, a fact recognized in the UK's 'In Terms of Zone A' (ITZA) valuation method. This chapter will look at the language of storefronts and the principles of their design.

The evolution of the storefront begins with the market stall of the Middle Ages, with the earliest shops being a partial enclosure of the stall. Until the fifteenth century, goods sold from shops would most likely have been sold through an open window to passing customers. As the value of goods and the size of transactions grew, there was undoubtedly a need to bring transacting inside to offer customers a safer and more comfortable environment in which to consider their purchase. Openings to the front of the store would have been protected by shutters and grilles but the development of glass technology in the mid-seventeenth century reinforced the notion of the sales being transacted within the store and no longer through a shuttered window.

By the middle of the eighteenth century, glazed storefronts as we know them today were the norm and they derived their design from the classical commercial architecture of the day with the terms for storefront components borrowed from the language of classism. As glass technology developed, so did the storefront, with tall plate glass sheets set between vertical mullions as found in Victorian storefronts from around the mid-nineteenth century. Further developments in metal technology saw the incorporation of cast iron and bronze as well as the opportunity to use the glazed ceramics characteristic of the Art Deco period. The twentieth century saw the development of large-format and curved glass, allowing for today's fully glazed and frameless façades.

COMPONENTS OF A STOREFRONT

Traditional storefronts, that is to say those that typically survive from the Victorian era, are derived from the language of classical architecture, adapted

One of London's finest surviving mid-Georgian storefronts built in the 1750s. Although no longer used as a store, the building has retailed groceries, silk and cigars at various times in its past.

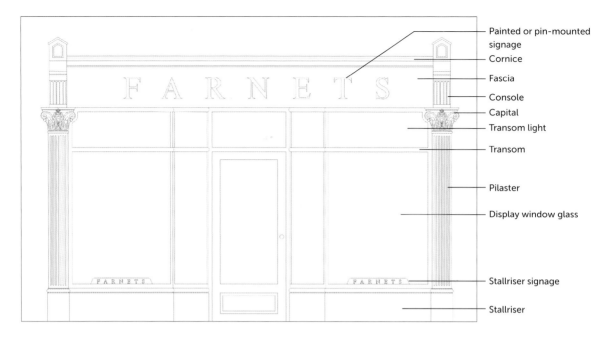

Traditional storefront components.

Painted or pin-mounted signage
Cornice
Fascia
Console
Capital
Transom light
Transom
Pilaster
Display window glass
Stallriser signage
Stallriser

in scale to the requirement of the nineteenth-century storekeeper. The display window is generally framed with columns or pilasters, over which sits the fascia. Below the display glass is the stallriser, a remnant from an earlier era when the window to the store or stall was closed with a hinged shutter that folded under the open window when the store was open. The decoration, column fluting, mouldings and other elements loosely reflect the chosen classical style and so we might find pilasters topped with Corinthian or Ionic consoles. The store's fascia was often designed to incorporate an awning box which closed flush to the fascia when retracted.

Whilst the language that describes the components of a modern storefront remains the same, contemporary storefronts are usually designed with a far higher percentage of glazing and with fewer columns to ensure that the view into the store is uninterrupted. To maximise the store's display windows, the stallriser is usually non-existent or reduced to little more than a deep section cill to the display window.

The Store Entrance

Unless the store is very large, it is unusual to access the store by more than one entrance. There are practical reasons for this, including the need to concentrate security on a single point, but also to help define the customer journey through the store with the appropriate way-finding and visual clues as to how the store is laid out.

The standard small storefront can take a variety of forms which vary in emphasis between the importance of the display window and the type of door opening.

Standard Door

The door opening sits in the same plane as the storefront. When glazed across the width of the storefront, this results in a clean uninterrupted design with good expanses of display window. This configuration is typical for high street stores but can

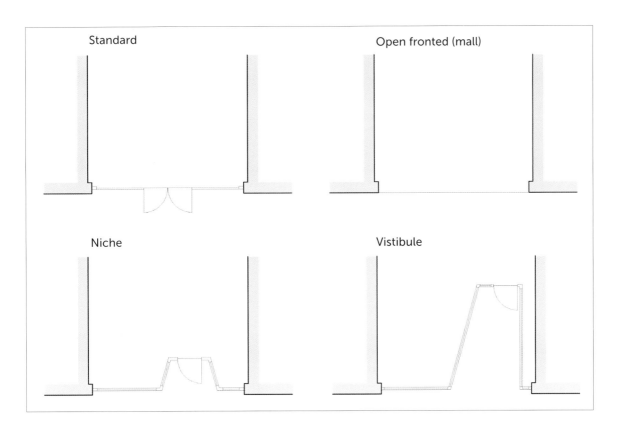

Typical store entrance types encountered in the high street or shopping mall.

Traditional central door between two display windows at Hermès, Luxembourg.

be problematic where doors open outwards into pedestrian traffic. For this reason, the loss of floor space required to create a niche doorway is worth considering.

Open Fronted

The store is open, with no display window or door. This is the arrangement typically found in shopping malls, the store being protected by means of a shutter when not trading. There is no display window as such, but often the necessity of the store layout will restrict access across the entire width of the storefront.

Open mall storefront, relying on shutters to secure the retail space out of hours. Samsonite, Täby Mall, Stockholm.

Niche entrance within arched storefront at Paul Smith, Coal Drops Yards, London.

Niche

The door sits in a niche, set back from the line of the storefront allowing space for the door to swing safely or to be left in the open position. The effect of creating a niche also serves to give the display windows more depth, emphasizing the door position.

Vestibule

This style is not commonly found in new developments because of the amount of selling space sacrificed to display windows and the amount of external circulation space required. The emphasis on display is heightened but, when merchandised well, the whole

storefront can become a brilliant advertisement for the store.

Is an Open-Door Policy Valid?

In a mall, it is relatively rare to enclose the front of the store but it is often the case in high street stores that the main doors are left open. Many retailers believe that closed doors discourage passing customers from entering their store and so it has long been held to be good practice to leave the door open, regardless of the weather conditions and the cost of doing so. The energy losses through maintaining an open-door policy are usually through cooling in the summer months or heating in the winter months. Notwithstanding the energy costs in pursuit of this policy, independent research carried out by Imperial College and King's College London on London's Regent Street in 2014 found that air pollution recorded in the stores tested could be significantly reduced by around one third by a closed-door policy during trading hours. The study demonstrated the value of a closed-door policy in areas of high air pollution, particularly to staff who are exposed to the condition throughout their working day. The retailer must therefore balance the need to encourage passing trade whilst addressing energy costs and the protection of staff from pollution.

Extensive display windows created by vestibule entrance at Cinderalla, Knokke-Heist, Belgium.

If open-door policies start to become less desirable and pressure against them builds from environmentally conscious consumers, then retailers may need to design stores to make them just as appealing to passing trade when the door is closed as when open. As retailers adapt stores to improve accessibility, automatically opening doors are becoming more common; when properly used, these effectively offer an open door on demand. Improvements should also be considered to sight lines through doors and storefronts so that the customer can see and understand what lies beyond the door from the street and is drawn in.

Signage

In almost all cases, whether high street, mall or pop-up kiosk, brands try to ensure that their name is clearly displayed and understood. In a busy location is it important that the store name or the brand's identity is clear to see and identifiable amongst many others. Traditionally the store's principal signage location is the fascia, the band of space that usually spans the width of the storefront and sits over the shop windows and the entrance. Because of its height, fascia signage offers the prospect of being seen from a distance by passing or approaching customers and as such it is appropriate that investment in high-quality fascia signage is made as it is a strong indicator of a brand's quality.

Fascia Signage

Painted Lettering

Typical of traditional storefront design, this type of signage can convey high quality with great simplicity if executed properly. The signage can be painted directly onto the fascia or on a separate sign which is mechanically fixed to the fascia. Whilst this simple design is unlikely to be bold enough in a mall environment, it may be a requirement if the store is located in a historic district or conservation area.

Pin-Mounted Lettering

Individual characters are mounted just off the surface of the fascia to create a sign with a small amount of visual depth. With the right choice of material for the lettering, this can be an effective and stylish solution, but it works best when there is enough of a 'field' of space around the letters to allow them to be seen to good effect.

Where signage is either painted or pin-mounted, it is often lit by light fittings directed on the fascia. Because the light fittings themselves are necessarily located close to the fascia, care must be taken not to create unusual and unintentional shadow effects, particularly where pin-mounted signage is used. The method of lighting varies from picture lights

Brewdog's simple yet very effective painted signage in Leeds, West Yorkshire.

Remote lighting of pin-mounted fascia signage for White Stuff, Leeds.

a patchy appearance. With the advent of smaller and more reliable LED light sources, this method has largely been superseded in favour of individual back-lit letters. This is similar in principle to back-lit fascia signage but with each character acting as an individual light box. This type of signage solution tends to work best on larger logos with fewer characters because of the challenge in wiring, mounting and maintaining a vast array of characters. Where the typeface or logo contains very small elements that can prove too small to accommodate even the smallest LED light source, halo-lit littering may be more effective.

mounted above the fascia to strip lighting running either above or below the fascia and often concealed in a trough. Whilst this method can be cumbersome, it can often find a place in schemes where the entire storefront is lit.

Unless there are specific requirements imposed by the landlord or the planning authority, most retailers will wish to illuminate the fascia signage so that it has the desired impact in the hours of darkness. Where illumination is required, there are several possible approaches, as considered below.

Halo-Lit Lettering

Unlike the other methods of illumination which seek to either direct an external light source onto the lettering or illuminate from within, halo lighting seeks to illuminate the space around the individual characters so that the characters themselves are seen in

Back-Lit Signage

In this case, the signage is illuminated from within or behind the sign, so that the sign is effectively a large light box. Traditionally the whole fascia would have been treated this way with banks of fluorescent tubes overlaid with a transparent facing material such as acrylic. Where this method is used and there are large areas of semi-transparency, it is important to ensure that the light source is evenly distributed to avoid

Nicely proportioned back-lit signage of individual letters at Aritzia, Hudson Yards, New York.

Acrylic-mounted halo lighting at Fendi, Hong Kong.

neon signage is no longer widely used in commercial situations as, whilst it is stylish, it offers limited colour choice and has a number of disadvantages. Neon signage is made of shaped glass tubes filled with neon, helium, xenon or krypton, with each gas producing a different colour light. The tubes are fragile and a single crack renders the whole tube broken. Neon lighting requires a high voltage which often means that a separate 'fireman's switch' for the sign's isolation is required. Fortunately, designers wishing to emulate the appearance of neon signage can use LED flexible strip lighting comprising LED chips in a waterproof translucent silicone cover; this can be easily cut and mounted.

silhouette or part silhouette. This method can be a useful means of introducing some illumination in situations where conservative or subtle lighting only is permitted. There are two approaches to this design. Where the individual characters are large enough to be formed of sheet metal with sufficient depth to accommodate a light source, these can be pin-mounted a small distance proud of the face of the façade, allowing the light to flood out and wash over the fascia around the edge of the character.

An increasingly popular method, particularly as it lends itself well to signs with small characters or intricate designs, is to use a layer of acrylic between the fascia and the signage material itself. The internal light source transmits itself through the perspex, giving a continuous solid glow to the back of the characters which gives the sign a sharply lit appearance.

Other Methods of Signage

Hanging and Blade Signs

Hanging signs have long been used by retailers to advertise their businesses and we are familiar with the pawnbroker's three gold balls or the barber's

Neon Signage

Neon signage can be both simple and stunning in its effect. True

Paul Smith neon hanging sign in Leeds, West Yorkshire.

Hanging and blade signs need not just mimic the store's fascia sign, as Taps & Baths demonstrate in Knokke-Heist, Belgium.

striped pole. Hanging signs are mounted on a frame, usually triangulated to the storefront with straps or struts for stability. Where illumination is required, picture lights mounted at the head of the sign are typical. Blade signs are the modern equivalent of the hanging sign and these are usually fixed at the same or a similar height to the fascia signage and cantilevered to project out from the storefront. Blade signs are often internally illuminated in ways similar to those described for fascia signs. Where permitted, both hanging and blade signs offer the retailer excellent visibility to potential customers approaching from the side, along a pavement or walkway. Designers should take note of the wind load on hanging and cantilevered designs and ensure that the sign is mounted at a sufficient height above passing pedestrians.

Stallriser Signage

The base of the display window can be an ideal location for smaller, secondary signage or brand name. A similar sign location is the base of a display window or vitrine.

Entrance Floor Signage

Names or logos set into the floor finish on the door threshold can be effective in delineating a brand from its neighbours.

Awnings

Awnings provide ample opportunity to display store logos or names. These are likely to work best when the awning is fixed and the graphic is permanently on display. (This topic is examined in greater detail below.)

Stallriser signage at Nespresso, Meadowhall, South Yorkshire.

The Kooples in Luxembourg use only the edge of the store's awnings to display the brand name.

Flags

Flags can be a decorative way to display a brand's name or logo. The traditional method is a façade-mounted flagpole that projects at 45 degrees to the horizontal. The flag is cut with a 45-degree sloping top so that it falls vertically from the pole. This presents the designer with a problem of fit if the brand name is long and so logos or graphics often make for a better design. Flags should be retained with guy ropes to prevent them tangling in high winds. On larger buildings, such as department stores or major flagship stores, a standard vertical flagpole and rectangular flag can be deployed.

Miscellaneous Details

If signage proves difficult to incorporate, designers might consider introducing the logo into architectural elements such as door handles or push plates, or into internal signage visible through the shop window.

Traditional quadrilateral flag designed for a 45-degree flagpole. Berry Brothers & Rudd Ltd, London.

Awnings

The broad design of retractable awnings remains unchanged since their advent in the late 1800s. The main element of the awning is a roller or drum around which the awning fabric is wound. The rollers of many awnings of the late Victorian and early Edwardian era are contained in boxes recessed into the fascia, although the retro-fitted awnings commonly fitted today roll into externally mounted aluminium boxes. The awning is extended and retracted by means of folding metal arms connected to the front of the awning. Various types of arm device have been used over the years, from arms that rise and fall on vertical bars mounted to the façade either side of the display window to concertina-type arms from which the awning is suspended. The use of awnings was commonplace in an era when there was no electric lighting or air conditioning and shopkeepers sought to control light and solar gain. Many storefronts of this era still retain the awning box, even if the actual awning has long been made redundant. The twenty-first century version of the awning relies on folding aluminium arms that lie under the awning itself. The awning is operated through electric motors which can be controlled remotely and, in some cases, it is linked to sensors that monitor sunlight and wind speed.

Fixed awnings are a cheaper option but without the possibility of retraction when required. The Dutch, or bonnet, blind extends in a semi-circular arc from the façade. The Dutch blind lacks the practicality of the traditional awning as it does not extend as far, and can appear overbearing and top-heavy due to its overall height. Fixed blinds afford some degree of solar shade but are otherwise mostly installed for decorative purposes. As we have seen in the description of fascia signage, the awning offers a good opportunity to display brand names and logos.

Elegant Rituals awnings perfectly frame the store's entrance, Luxembourg.

Display furniture need not always comprise boxes and rails, as this shoe table resembling a split meteorite shows. Forty Five Ten, Hudson Yards, New York.

Chapter Six

Display and Fixturing

MILLWORK

Store display fittings generally fall into one of two groups, either perimeter or free-standing. These are supplemented with loose furniture and operational fixtures, notably the point of sale cash desk. The design and installation of these shop fittings requires careful consideration, not only to enhance the overall appearance of the store and the customer experience, but also to display the store's merchandise to best advantage.

Millwork or Joinery?

As the use of American terminology has become more prevalent in store design, the use of the word 'millwork' has become commonplace. Traditionally, 'millwork' referred to pieces of woodwork that were produced and finished in a mill and so came to mean generally industrially produced woodwork furniture pieces, doors, panels and so on. Today the term is more likely to refer to any manufactured joinery pieces commissioned for the display of a store's merchandise, be they mass-produced or to a bespoke design. Furthermore, millwork no longer refers just to pieces made from wood but also to metal and glass and combinations of these materials. As far as store design is now concerned, 'millwork' tends to be the all-encompassing term for shopfitting joinery.

Perimeter Fixtures

Most retailers can ill afford the luxury of a blank wall in their store. Although the drama created by an artwork can be used to great effect, the reality is that the perimeter wall is where most retailers look to display product. Perimeter fixtures can be broadly described as either carrying hanging product or shelf product (or a combination of the two), and each requires a different approach to their design. Where a simple and economic solution is required, an off-the-shelf (if the pun may be excused) system can be considered.

Perimeter of traditionally detailed and built-in display millwork at Kate Spade, London. (Photo: Hyphen)

Slatwall and Twin Slot Systems

Slatwall systems were first patented in the US in 1966 as 'article display board' and have been widely developed as a generic perimeter fixturing system since as it allows the display of a wide variety of product using standard components. The system usually comprises MDF wall panels of 1.2m × 2.4m with horizontal channels at 70–80mm centres. Once the panels have been suitably mounted to the perimeter wall, components such as shelves, hangers and baskets and so on can be slotted on to a channel to create the desired display. Where heavily loaded fixtures are predicted, the channels may be reinforced with aluminium inset channels. A similar flexible system of display is the cage wall, in which a metal cage or mesh replaces the slatwall board, with components clipped onto the bars of the mesh.

The slatwall panels should be fixed to timber studwork or a plywood interlayer, rather than direct to the perimeter wall. This is to ensure that the mounting surface is absolutely flat. Once suitable studwork or a plywood interlayer has been constructed, the slatwall panels can be mechanically fixed with screws concealed in the joints between panels. The panels are usually self-finished in a variety of materials such as laminate, wood veneer, mirror and metallic and other decorative finishes.

Twin slot systems comprise vertical steel channels into which are cut multiple slots at fixed heights. Shelf brackets and other components are clipped into the slots which are held stable under the load imposed by the shelf. These systems are usually supplied self-finished and can easily be incorporated into perimeter or mid-floor fixtures.

Bespoke Perimeter Display

The degree to which the perimeter elements are incorporated into the wall and ceiling is a key consideration when designing millwork for the perimeter of a store. There are two extremes of design: the wholly built-in display and the entirely free-standing display. In deciding which design direction to follow, the designer should consider a number of possible constraints inherent in each approach.

Gondola unit with adjustable shelves on twin slot brackets designed to carry considerable levels of stock. Zurheide in Düsseldorf.

Ralph Lauren's highly ordered and carefully coordinated arrangement of built-in perimeter display. Knokke-Heist, Belgium. (Photo: Hyphen)

Built-In Display

This design produces an ordered display, where the millwork is usually framed by the interior architecture of the store. To achieve the desired outcome, a high degree of coordination is required between the floor and ceiling design, as well as with the enclosing wall in which the built-in display sits. Whilst the coordination between millwork and shell poses some challenges there are particular advantages to this approach. The voids created between the display millwork and the shell easily allow services to be run around the perimeter of the store. In addition, because this approach effectively creates a room within a room, the condition of the existing perimeter grey box is less critical. As a counterpoint, however, once the millwork dimensions have been set, there is very little opportunity to vary the shell dimensions if any issues are discovered on site that throw out the anticipated dimensions.

Built-in display with top illumination concealed by pelmet. Ralph Lauren, Knokke-Heist, Belgium. (Photo: Hyphen)

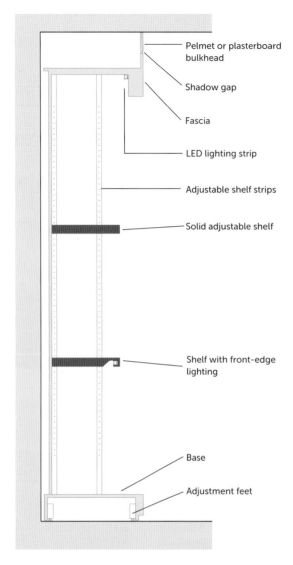

Built-in display millwork detail.

Labels in the diagram:
- Pelmet or plasterboard bulkhead
- Shadow gap
- Fascia
- LED lighting strip
- Adjustable shelf strips
- Solid adjustable shelf
- Shelf with front-edge lighting
- Base
- Adjustment feet

Free-Standing Display

Free-standing perimeter displays tend to be more forgiving on sites where there is little dimensional tolerance. Free-standing millwork produces a more loose-fit aesthetic, but greater consideration must therefore be given to the form and finish of the floor and ceiling as well as the enclosing wall. Although the aesthetic is informal, free-standing pieces may demand carefully coordinated services connections, particularly where the millwork includes integral lighting.

Mid-Floor Fixtures

Mid-floor fixtures are seen in the round and so consideration must be given to their appearance from all sides. Without the possibility of mounting to a perimeter wall, mid-floor fixtures must be designed with stability in mind, which can be a challenge when the fixture is tall or likely to be subjected to dynamic lateral loads such as those imposed by a heavily loaded hanging rail. Lighter fixture pieces can be set on castors or wheels to allow them to be moved, thus introducing a degree of flexibility in the store's layout. Where mid-floor fixtures require a power supply for lighting, audio-visual display or point of sale, this is usually provided by means of a floor box located directly under the fixture. Very careful setting out of floor boxes is required, usually at the

Extensive free-standing display composed mostly of hanging rails; the clamp and tube design helps structure the space. Lane Crawford, Hong Kong.

Free-standing display with lit shelves located in niche at Bottega Veneta, Alsterhaus, Hamburg. (Photo: Hyphen)

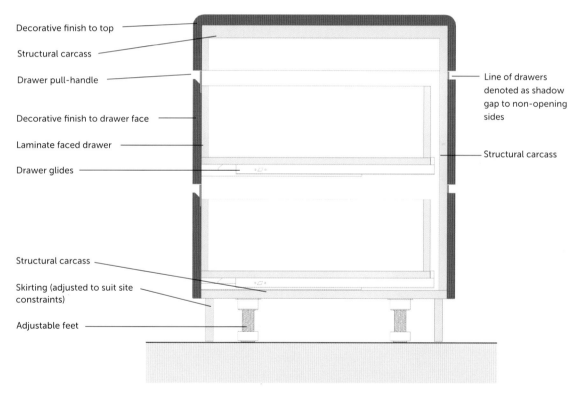

Decorative finish to top

Structural carcass

Drawer pull-handle

Decorative finish to drawer face

Laminate faced drawer

Drawer glides

Line of drawers denoted as shadow gap to non-opening sides

Structural carcass

Structural carcass

Skirting (adjusted to suit site constraints)

Adjustable feet

Section details of mid-floor millwork piece.

time when the floor is screeded. This is to ensure that when the mid-floor fixtures are located in their final position, they site directly over the floor box.

Where power is required to a table and the cable route runs through one of the table legs, an even more precise alignment of cable and furniture is required. In this instance it is not usually practical to supply power via a floor box and so the power cable is run as a spur which can be isolated remotely.

Elegant fragrance table with drawers to carry stock and a back-lit top to illuminate glass bottles. Abercrombie & Fitch at Eston Town Center, Ohio.

Simple but effective free-standing display tables allowing the merchandise to be seen against a backdrop. Burberry at Selfridges, London. (Photo: Hyphen)

Millwork Manufacture

Millwork is usually tendered using the store designer's design intent drawings. These show the key dimensions, materials and finishes but not necessarily the precise detail of the joints within the millwork or how components are assembled. The reason for this is that millwork manufacturers will have their own methods of forming, milling and assembling in their workshops and so it makes little sense for the store designer to attempt to second-guess them. The millwork manufacturer will prepare their own manufacture and assembly drawings, sometimes referred to as rod drawings. Rod drawings were traditionally 1:1 drawings of the millwork created to verify the setting out of the final fabrication, but with the advent of scalable CAD drawings and computer-aided manufacture these are rarely encountered now. The store designer checks the manufacturer's drawings and mock-ups or sample pieces might be prepared before the manufacturing stage is approved.

Where the millwork is to be built into a wall niche or has to otherwise fit a precise dimension, the millwork manufacturer will visit to survey the site. Depending on the type of millwork, the survey or dimension check will take place at a time between when the general contractor has completed the site setting out to the point when the white box shell has been completed.

The majority of millwork is fabricated using a softwood or MDF carcass which is finished or over-clad in the desired surface material. With the exception of very small runs of handmade bespoke joinery, most millwork carcassing is produced using computer-aided machining which ensures a high degree of speed and precision at a reasonable cost. The cut pieces are then either fully assembled by hand on the bench or partially assembled for completion on site. The latter method is particularly common where millwork pieces are large, require building in or have to be shipped a long distance.

Facing materials such as veneers and laminates can be applied either before or after the carcass components are cut and, depending on the design, hardwood edges or lipping might be applied prior to the laying of the veneer to give the finished piece the appearance of solid wood. Other facing materials include solid surface acrylic sheet materials such as Corian or Avonite which can be thermoformed to produce curved sections. Sprayed finishes are

When commissioning millwork, mock-up pieces and samples should always be sought, both as proof of concept and as a quality check prior to production. (Photo: Hyphen)

Inside a well-managed millwork production facility. Computer-aided manufacturing ensures both speed and accuracy at d3 Design & Display Ltd, Elland, West Yorkshire. (Photo: d3 Design & Display Ltd)

also widely used and include polyurethane paint, polyester lacquer and liquid metal sprays such as VeroMetal.

Most well-resourced manufactures will be able to manufacture everything in-house but where millwork pieces include significant amounts of glass, metal-work or upholstery, these are usually subcontracted out to other firms.

The final assembly might include the installation of hardware such as shelf support strips, drawer slides, handles and hinges. Where lighting or power is included in the pieces, these are installed and tested prior to dispatch to site.

Loose Furniture

Chairs, occasional tables and other furniture pieces might be sourced from suppliers' standard ranges or manufactured by the millwork manufacturer. When sourcing loose furniture from standard product ranges, sample pieces should be obtained prior to ordering to verify their suitability.

Upholstered millwork forming an impressive island of seating from which to buy shoes. Forty Five Ten, Hudson Yards, New York.

CASE STUDY: SELFRIDGES WOMEN'S SHOE GALLERIES

In 2003, Canadian retailer Galen Weston bought out Selfridges and Co. (hitherto listed on the Stock Exchange) and began an ambitious programme of work to modernise and improve the Selfridges stores in London, Birmingham and Manchester. The first remodelled space in London, the Wonder Room, opened in 2007 and the process of re-building has continued since, culminating in David Chipperfield's project to create a new accessories hall and eastern entrance which was completed in 2018. During this period, Jamie Fobert Architects have designed new departments within the store including the Women's Shoe Galleries, Womenswear and Men's Designer Street Room. The Shoe Galleries were originally completed in 2010 and subsequently remodelled by Jamie Fobert Architects eight years later in response to the changes to the store arising from the Chipperfield scheme. The Shoe Galleries are located in the store's north-eastern corner in a part of the store that was added to Gordon Selfridge's original concept from the 1930s onwards.

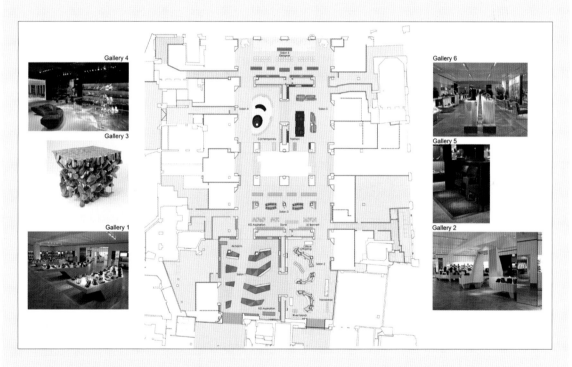

Architect's plan of the 2010 Women's Shoe Galleries showing six salons, each with different themes, forms and materials. (Photo: Jamie Fobert Architects, Sue Barr and Olivier Hess)

Unlike many department stores, Selfridges Women's Shoes is not a large, single-volume space but rather a collection of six separate salons, laid out *enfilade*. This allows two principal sight lines to run through the entire width of the store, from Oxford Street to the mews running parallel at the back of the store. Jamie Fobert Architects conceived the six salons as galleries, each containing different themes, materials and products. Around the edges of the galleries are clustered a number of brand concessions chosen to complement the theme of each gallery. The styles and price points range from trainers to exclusives from the world's most famous shoe designers. The architectural concept for the display furniture responds to this variety through the selection and use of materials, using more informal, industrial finishes for casual wear and more traditional, classic methods and materials for formal wear.

Throughout the Shoe Galleries the floor is French oak, laid in a variety of patterns but with a distinctive herringbone pattern to demarcate the walkways. All of the galleries share an uncluttered ceiling, a sense of space and long sight lines through the building. Beyond these shared characteristics, the display furniture for each gallery is distinct, with bespoke fixtures using materials that might not be expected to be seen in a department store. In the original scheme these included the following materials in juxtaposition; clay and steel, concrete and rubber, velvet and shards of glass plus cracked oak and pewter.

Oak and pewter were utilized in a number of ways in Gallery 3. Oak blocks with saw marks and natural splits and cracks were filled or covered with pewter and the resultant plinths grouped into mini-landscapes. The central display tables in this gallery are some of the most striking in the department. Original wooden shoe lasts that were salvaged from cobblers' workshops were sliced and set in molten pewter to create a remarkable, fossil-like surface on which to exhibit shoes. The architect developed a supporting structure of shoe lasts and metal rods, experimenting with mock-ups and models before the final manufacture was handed over to MDM Props.

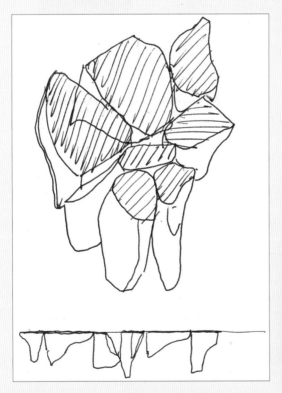

Architect's concept sketch for the shoe last and pewter table for the Women's Shoe Galleries. (Photo: Jamie Fobert Architects)

Architect's model used to develop the shoe last table concept for the Women's Shoe Galleries. (Photo: Jamie Fobert Architects)

Fabrication at MDM Props of the Women's Shoe Galleries shoe last table. (Photo: Jamie Fobert Architects)

Women's Shoe Galleries shoe last table merchandised in store. (Photo: Olivier Hess)

Alabaster plinths in Gallery 6 of the Women's Shoe Galleries. (Photo: Andrew Meredith)

Gallery 6 was designed to display the most exclusive brands and so the architect sought to convey a greater sense of luxury. This was achieved through a less dense arrangement of furniture and merchandise, which allows the shoes to be displayed as if they were treasures or works of art.

To exhibit the shoes, a fleet of forty-two beautiful stone plinths were commissioned. These are carved from naturally veined alabaster, translucent under the bright store lighting, which makes the plinths instantly recognizable as bespoke, luxury furnishings. The translucency and intricacy of the alabaster emphasizes the contrast between the solidity of the dark steel shelves and the sophistication of the black horsehair and silk used as shelf-lining fabrics.

The manufacture of the plinths was entrusted to stone masons Marmi & Granito who cut blocks of quarried alabaster into the plinth shape before shaping and honing the stone to Jamie Fobert Architects' design.

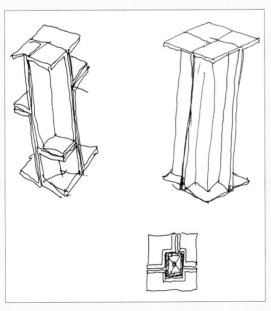

Architect's concept sketch for the alabaster plinths in Gallery 6. (Photo: Jamie Fobert Architects)

Alabaster blocks being cut by Marmi & Granito to form plinths for the Women's Shoe Galleries. (Photo: Jamie Fobert Architects)

Alabaster plinths with merchandise in Gallery 6 of the Women's Shoe Galleries. (Photo: Olivier Hess)

In 2018, Jamie Fobert Architects gave the Shoe Galleries a fresh look, with new design concepts and a greater emphasis on sustainability. In Gallery 2, the original 'green dragon' display piece was replaced with mid-floor display tables made of fragmented and interlocking grey and white sheets; similar forms are used for the perimeter shelves. The material used is derived from 100 per cent recycled plastic, primarily yoghurt pots and plastic packaging.

Alabaster blocks being shaped by Marmi & Granito for the Women's Shoe Galleries. (Photo: Jamie Fobert Architects)

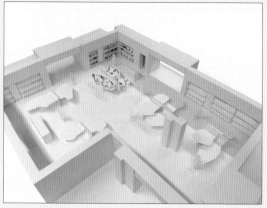

Architect's model of 2018 scheme for Women's Shoe Gallery 2. (Photo: Jamie Fobert Architects)

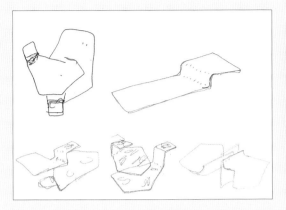

Architect's 2018 concept sketches for display furniture for Women's Shoe Gallery 2. (Photo: Jamie Fobert Architects)

Gallery 2 of the Women's Shoe Galleries, 2018 scheme. (Photo: Olivier Hess)

A major new addition to the Shoes Galleries is the new sneaker wall in Gallery 3 offering a striking display for Selfridges' extensive selection of women's sneakers. Vertical bands of stainless steel have been folded to form individual display shelves. The vapour-blasted finish of stainless steel on multiple facets creates soft reflections, picking up the bright colours of sneakers. The overall effect is of a wave or ripple along the shoe gallery perimeter.

Gallery 3 sneaker wall of the Women's Shoe Galleries, 2018 scheme. (Photo: Olivier Hess)

It is interesting to see how Jamie Fobert Architects' original scheme from 2010 has evolved over the course of eight years. The original concept of light, linked galleries that afford long sight lines and are unified by an oak floor that flows throughout has certainly stood the test of time. As the 'exhibits' in the galleries have been replaced, the architect has explored new forms and materials but still with the inventive shape-making and exquisite attention to detail that informed the original project.

DISPLAY AND VISUAL MERCHANDISING

Architect and author Barry Maitland described visual merchandising as the art of displaying and promoting the store's merchandise 'in which the character of the setting is seen to be vastly more important than, say, the price-competitiveness of the product'.

The spheres of visual merchandising (VM) and store design overlap considerably, but if a distinction needs to be made, the store designer will be more concerned with the internal architecture and those static elements that contribute to defining the store's interior. The visual merchandiser may also contribute to the design of the layout of the store, but with a greater focus on how this is influenced by product and how the customer encounters the product. Well-designed display furniture is usually a collaborative effort between the store designer, with their understanding of materials, ergonomics and procurement, and the visual merchandiser who better understands the merchandise, the product density and how to stage products for display purposes.

Display Windows

Visiting customers first encounter visual merchandising in the store's display windows. Department stores around the world have become justifiably famous for their window displays and particularly at Christmas, a tradition that dates back to Macy's animated displays of the nineteenth century. The traditional display window comprises an enclosed space open to the front only, although open-backed or partially enclosed variants are also found. The advantage of an enclosed window is that the surrounding walls act as a backdrop against which to set off the display.

Attention-grabbing VM in Panerai's pop-up store at Harbour City Mall, Hong Kong.

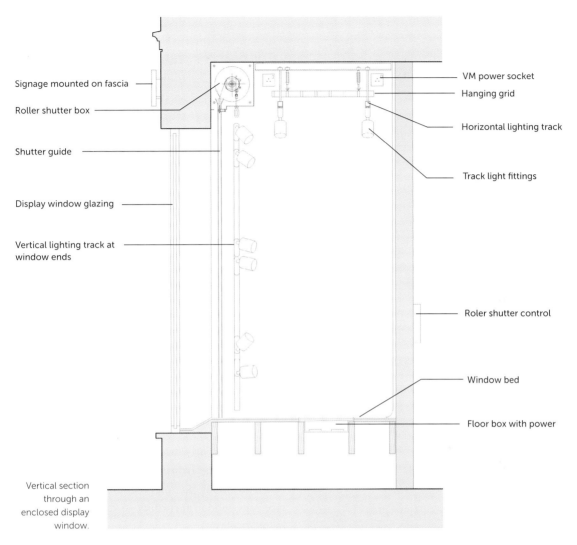

Signage mounted on fascia

Roller shutter box

Shutter guide

Display window glazing

Vertical lighting track at window ends

VM power socket

Hanging grid

Horizontal lighting track

Track light fittings

Roler shutter control

Window bed

Floor box with power

Vertical section through an enclosed display window.

Powerful visual merchandising adds interest to an otherwise simple display of mannequins in an enclosed display window at Aritzia, Hudson Yards, New York.

Changes of season, in-store promotions and the need to create interest ensure that window displays are changed with regularity. A well-designed display window can make the process of change easier and the end result more effective. Consideration must be given to well-placed lighting and electric sockets. Very often VM displays require components to be hung from the ceiling and a hanging grid in the soffit of the window can facilitate this.

Open-backed window at Neiman Marcus, Hudson Yards, New York requires the visual merchandiser to consider the effectiveness of the display in the round.

Visual Merchandising Tools

There are a number of VM tools which, whilst not necessarily the responsibility of the store designer, should be considered in the store design. It is important therefore to have a working knowledge of VM tools and installations so that provision can be made in the design for them: for example, designing good lighting to the product shelves might not in itself create suitable lighting to show a mannequin well. Where the retailer uses video display and light boxes, these require power and data connections to be provided and incorporated into the overall store design.

Mannequins

Mannequins are available in a wide range of styles ranging from highly abstract to realistic; they must be selected for the appropriate size and gender according to the type of apparel being displayed.

Well-lit window display at Maje, Luxembourg.

Realistic full-body mannequins, Euroshop, Düsseldorf.

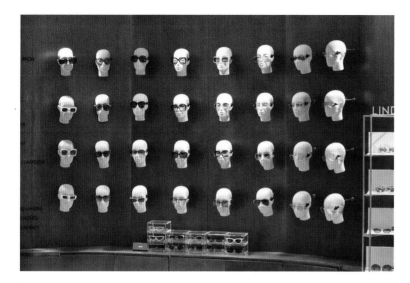

Clever use of head mannequins to create a multi-brand sunglasses wall at Lane Crawford, Hong Kong.

A large-format video display lights up the night at the K11 Art Mall, Hong Kong.

Video Display

The use of video display in retail has developed rapidly as large-format video screen technology has advanced. Whilst the hardware is easily understood and installed, the retailer should be certain that the content can be maintained and refreshed. Rather than the use of video, the traditional light box with still images can provide a more robust and more easily updated solution.

Art and Interactive Installations

Some stores, and particularly well-resourced brands such as Nike, dedicate a lot of their flagship store space to intriguing and informative displays, entertaining interactive activities and games. Such significant interventions of experience-led retail are considered from the outset of the store's design, with flexible spaces included within the concept which can be periodically refreshed.

Inventive brand storytelling that extends through the store and hangs in the stairwell of Nike House of Innovation, New York.

Coordinated service zones ensure an orderly,
open ceiling design at Zurheide in Düsseldorf. GEMÜSE

FRÜCHTE

Chapter Seven

Building Services and Lighting

WHILST THE STORE'S SERVICES ARE FREquently concealed out of sight in the completed project, they are nevertheless a vital component in ensuring that the store can operate and function properly, specifically that the store's environment is comfortable, healthy and safe. The services design must respond to the external climate that prevails outside the store as well as constraints imposed by the store's architecture, including available space through which to run services or locate plant and equipment. The services engineer also has a leading role to play to ensure that the design is sustainable, being able to offer advice on energy use, operational (running) costs and whole life cycle costs. In the majority of retail projects, the services design comprises a number of separate disciplines which must be coordinated with one another as well as with the main architectural and fit-out works. It is essential therefore that services design is considered early in the design of the store, otherwise the designer may struggle to adapt their concept to accommodate the necessities of ductwork, cable ways, plant and equipment.

BUILDING SERVICES

The MEP Team

The various disciplines of services design can be known collectively by different acronyms, but generally refer to the same disciplines:

MEP: mechanical, electrical and plumbing (or public health)

HVAC: heating, ventilation and air conditioning

M&E: mechanical and electrical

The service engineer's brief is to create systems that can be controlled to ensure the comfort and health of the store's occupants. The influences on the individual to be considered are wide and include visual and acoustic stimuli as well as the more obvious factors of temperature and air quality. How individuals perceive comfort is subjective and everyone has different tolerances to high or low temperature or noise levels. Nevertheless, useful guidance on appropriate standards is published by the Chartered Institution of Building Services Engineers (CIBSE).

There is unlikely to be a standard design solution for every project, even where a brand is repeating a design concept of a similar size across several sites. The following factors should be investigated at the outset of the project as they are likely to influence the design of the services.

	Customary winter operative temperatures	Customary summer operative temperatures (air conditioned buildings)	Air-supply rate (litres/ second/ person)	Filtration grade	Noise criterion §			Maintained illuminance
					nr	dBA	dBC	
Retail	19–21°C	21–25°C	10	F5–F7	35–40	40–45	65–70	500 Lux
Office	21–23°C	22–25°C	10	F5–F7	30	35	60	500 Lux

Extract from CIBSE Environmental Design Guide A showing recommended comfort criteria:
§ = suggested maximum permissible background noise levels generated by building services installations; nr = the noise rating that takes into account the frequency content of the noise; dBA, dBC = decibel levels when measured though filters that allow mid-range frequencies (A) or high and low frequencies (C) to be measured.

MEP Design Considerations

Site Location and Aspect

In the UK, comprehensive data on the average monthly temperature in a given location is available from the Meteorological Office and similar advice is available locally around the world. In the northern hemisphere, site-specific factors (such a large area of south-facing glazing that can give rise to solar gain) should also be considered when determining the project's services requirements. For example, the level of solar gain could be significant in a high street location but negligible or non-existent in a mall location.

Architectural Constraints

As well as headroom requirements for the path of horizontal services, consideration must be given to vertical service penetrations where the site comprises multiple floors. Ideally, plant rooms or plant zones should be identified and confirmed early in the design to avoid unnecessary design changes as the design develops. In the early stages of the design, the building services can be sized based on rule-of-thumb calculations and established practice. In many shopping mall locations, the landlord is responsible for supplying the cooling, fresh air and power circuits from which the store's own systems feed, for example local ductwork and supply grilles in the sales area. Where the site is

a self-contained unit or in a high street location, it is more common to identify an external location where air-conditioning plant can be located, usually in the form of external condenser units. The size and suitability of external plant areas should be verified early in the design. Planning consent is usually required from the statutory authority because of constraints on plant noise levels and appearance. There may be a necessity, therefore, to undertake a noise survey and prepare noise calculations for submission with the application.

Achieving Comfort Through Design

The CIBSE guidance provides a helpful starting point from which to begin sizing the services installation. Whilst CIBSE provides separate data for different uses, it understandably does not distinguish between types of brands or store designs. A key part of the services design brief is to establish the store's likely occupancy level (that is to say, the number of people in the store at any given time) which will vary according to trade patterns. The statutory guidance available on occupancy concerns itself with life safety: for example, the Building Regulations Approved Document B2 on Fire Safety caps occupancy at $2m^2$ per person for most stores. This level of occupancy is unlikely to be encountered in most situations, although exceptions might occur during busy sales

External condenser units compete for space in this London lightwell. Ideally a dedicated plant area should be provided to facilitate maintenance access and to ensure the soundproofing of equipment.

The calm interior of Fortnum & Mason, London. Services have been carefully incorporated with the degree of intricacy demanded by a building that is over 100 years old. (Photo: Stefan Reimschuessel)

or promotion periods. It may be wholly uneconomic to design services to accommodate these rare periods of maximum capacity or for extremes in seasonal temperature changes. Nevertheless, if there is an acknowledgement that the temperature of the store's interior may rise above the recommended levels in certain circumstances it is important to quantify this and perhaps identify from the outset any temporary measures that may be required to mitigate the consequences of extreme periods. For example, a brand may not like the use of solar blinds in display windows but may accept such a measure to reduce solar gain for a few days in the height of the summer.

Having established the peak heating and cooling demand for specified occupancies and accounting for seasonal gains and losses, the plant and equipment can be sized. The services engineer's design must also consider the possibility of additional heat gains from lighting, display screens and other electrical equipment in the store. Having established the initial design through rule of thumb and benchmarking, the developed design is then tested by calculation, dynamic thermal modelling or computational fluid dynamics.

Temperature Control

In common with most commercial environments, the modern retail store is cooled by means of an air-conditioning system. In all but extremely large buildings or locations that form part of a shopping mall, a system of separate external condenser units and internal evaporator units are used: this system is known as a split refrigerant heat pump system. This has a number of advantages over larger refrigerant heat pump systems or systems using chilled water and ducted air. Firstly, it is scalable, allowing it to be adapted to suit the changing needs of the store. Secondly, the physical intervention required to install the system is less significant as the circuit between condenser and evaporator comprises small-bore pipework that transmits the cooling medium, in most cases a chemical refrigerant. The challenge for the designer is to identify a suitable route between the condenser, which is usually located in an external plant area, and the evaporator which is contained in a fan coil unit (or FCU) located close to the point of delivery of the conditioned air. In addition to the cooling requirement is the need to provide the store with fresh air. In all but the smallest stores which might be able to rely on natural ventilation, fresh air is ducted into the store as part of a circuit that draws out stale air to ensure that the air is continually replenished.

Refrigerant Heat Pump System

In the cooling mode, chemical refrigerant is pumped around a closed system of small-bore pipes and arrives at the external condenser unit warm, having picked up heat from the store's interior. The refrigerant is then cooled as it passes through the condenser by air

blown onto coils within the unit. The heat recovered is released to the surrounding air and the refrigerant returns to the store again via the small-bore pipe circuit. In the store the cooled refrigerant reaches an evaporator contained within an FCU and a similar exchange of heat occurs. Fresh air is blown over the coils of the evaporator containing the refrigerant, cooling the air, whilst the refrigerant picks up the excess warmth in the store. The circuit then repeats, with the refrigerant continuously circulated between the condenser and the evaporator of the FCU. The system described above can operate in the reverse cycle to provide a heating mode. In this case, the coil within the FCU provides heating to the store whilst the condenser releases cooler air to the surrounding air. Refrigerant heat pump systems are fairly flexible, with one or more condenser units serving multiple internal evaporators and with variations on the number and location of FCUs all possible. This type of system is therefore widely used in store design. We have only discussed simple cooling and heating so far, but by varying the flow of the refrigerant around the circuit, it is possible to create separate zones within the retail space that can be heated or cooled at different times or to different temperature levels. Heat recovery, where exhaust heat from one area is reused to warm other areas, is also possible, and can contribute to energy savings.

Fresh Air Supply

The supply and extraction of fresh air is controlled by an air-handling unit (or AHU). External air is pumped through the AHU where it is filtered and temperature controlled. It can also be adjusted for humidity although this is less common in retail applications. The conditioned air is ducted to the FCU, but not usually connected to it because the air entering the FCU is a mix of fresh air and air that is recirculated in the room. The FCU then cools or warms the air before delivering it via ducts to supply grilles, usually located in the ceiling of the retail space.

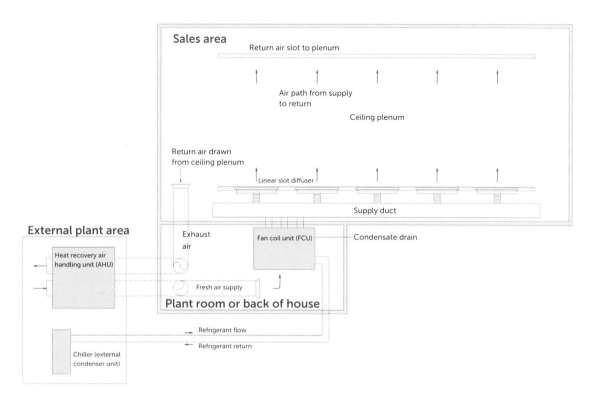

Sales area

Return air slot to plenum

Air path from supply to return

Ceiling plenum

Return air drawn from ceiling plenum

Linear slot diffuser

Supply duct

External plant area

Exhaust air

Fan coil unit (FCU)

Condensate drain

Heat recovery air handling unit (AHU)

Fresh air supply

Plant room or back of house

Refrigerant flow

Refrigerant return

Chiller (external condenser unit)

Diagram of typical refrigerant heat pump system.

The fresh air supply circuit is completed through the removal of the stale air via return air ductwork that is pumped out of the room by the AHU. Where the ceiling is open, return air grilles are attached to the ductwork and distributed across the ceiling to ensure adequate air flow. A more common detail where the store design uses a suspended ceiling is to create an air plenum in the ceiling void. In this case, the grille drawing the stale air into the duct is located in the ceiling void. The draw from the AHU creates a negative pressure in the plenum which draws stale air from the room through slots or grilles in the ceiling. Stale air in the plenum then enters the return air duct and is exhausted by the AHU.

Heat recovery air-handling unit in roof plant area. (Photo: Hyphen)

Evaporator Fan Coil Units

These are self-contained units, often ceiling-mounted but wall-mounted models are also available. The units contain all the required coils, fans and grilles to deliver the cooled or warmed air and the return air path is back to the same unit. Because the designer must accept the manufacturer's design and hence the appearance of the cassette unit, these units are probably more suited to office use or, in our case, back of house heating and cooling. They are seen in some smaller stores, but the impression is always that the store designer has had to surrender a large part of the ceiling design to the mechanical engineer. They are, however, cheaper and very compact.

Grille Options

Whilst the amount of free area through which the delivered air passes must be sized correctly, the main consideration in selecting and detailing grilles is likely to be aesthetic. The designer can usually decide between surface-mounted, recessed or concealed.

Concealed grilles can be particularly effective when located and hidden in troughs or slots. A well-designed scheme produces an effective heating and cooling system that remains unobtrusive and does not draw the eye from the rest of the store.

Care should not only be taken to coordinate the ductwork with lighting, sprinkler heads, cables and other ceiling devices, but also to recognize the requirements for access. Where the services are primarily located in a plasterboard ceiling, access must be considered for maintenance, repair and replacement: for example, the manufacturers of FCUs recommend that the filters are cleaned as often as every two weeks, particularly in a dusty or polluted environment. A suitably located access hatch to allow this for each unit is therefore required. Other access points may be required to allow for the adjustment of volume control dampers or the periodic testing and resetting of fire dampers.

Where the introduction of access hatches cannot be avoided, these can be made flush-mounted using proprietary systems of frames and doors so that they are as unobtrusive as possible.

Evaporator fan coil unit in open ceiling design, showing ducted fresh air supply. Wolf & Badger, Coal Drops Yard, London.

An open ceiling design where a grid of slotted channel allows total flexibility in the location of lighting and other ceiling devices. Nike House of Innovation, New York.

Safety Systems

Sprinklers

The requirement for sprinklers varies according to the nature of the building in which the store is located, the adopted fire strategy and building code considerations. Retail fit-out in department stores, shopping malls and transport hubs will certainly include sprinkler systems, whereas there are often no requirements for sprinklers in smaller high street stores.

When planning a store in one of the environments where sprinklers are required, it is usually the case that the landlord provides a sprinkler water supply or a branch from which to complete the installation. It is very often the case that the design and installation of the sprinkler system must be undertaken by an approved company so that the landlord maintains design and installation integrity for the entire system. Fortunately, sprinkler systems are relatively simple in principle and their design requirements are not often a significant constraint on the overall ceiling design. Sprinklers work through a system of pre-charged pipes that contain water from an independent circuit that is unaffected by other demands for water. This is maintained under pump pressure via a central pump serving the whole building. The charged pipes terminate in a temperature-sensitive head. One type of head is made from a glass bulb containing a liquid that, in the event of a fire, expands at a given temperature to break the bulb. Alternatively, the head can be a fusible link comprising a two-part metal element that is fused with a heat-sensitive alloy. At the crucial temperature, the alloy releases and the metal elements separate, which causes the head to open. Once the bulb has broken or the fusible link has failed, the pressurized water escapes and sprays the surrounding area with extinguishing water. A deflector at the end of the head spreads the water in a radial pattern. Because the sprinkler head is fixed and cannot be directed to the seat of a fire, the sprinkler heads must be arranged so as to cover the entire area being protected. Bulkheads, internal partitions and other obstructions can leave some floor areas unprotected and this can lead to the requirement for additional heads. Other factors that influence the design of the sprinkler system are the ceiling height and the anticipated fire load.

The sprinkler heads themselves are necessarily functional; where working with a prescribed sprinkler system, the designer may be forced to accept the heads offered, including the deflector colour. Where permitted, it may be possible to use concealed sprinkler heads. The appearance of this type is as a flush-mounted disk in the ceiling. The disc can be coloured to suit the surrounding ceiling and therefore made unobtrusive. A concealed head plate is designed to fail at a lower temperature than the main head, allowing the sprinkler head to activate unobstructed once the trigger temperature is reached.

Automatic Fire Detection

Before a fire reaches a point where the sprinkler system is activated, the automatic fire detection system should have ensured that alarms have been sounded and the premises safely evacuated. The detection system comprises a control panel to which detection devices are attached, either by current-carrying cables or wirelessly. The detection devices can be specified to detect for heat or smoke using whichever of several methods will best suit the environment in which they are installed. As well as automatic detection, manual call points or break-glass units are installed at final exit points to allow personnel to sound the alarm themselves. Once the control panel receives the detectors' signals, it activates the sounding of alarms, bells or voice messages. Activating the alarm may also trigger the operation of smoke ventilation, the dropping of smoke curtains or the release of fire doors.

A wired automatic fire detection system can be described as addressable or non-addressable. In an addressable system every connected device has a unique address, so that when a fire is detected, the control panel is able to identify the precise location of the alert. With a non-addressable system, the control panel can identify only which circuit has been activated. On larger buildings, however, the wiring is divided into zones so that the approximate location can nevertheless be identified.

Wireless systems are powered by batteries in the detector and communicate with the control panel via signals transmitted across radio bandwidth. The heads are addressable and the lack of wiring mean that they lend themselves to temporary locations or to situations where cabling is to be avoided, such as historic interiors where the building fabric cannot be altered.

Heat Detectors

Heat detectors use either single or dual thermistors, which are a type of resistor whose resistance is dependent on temperature. Thus an increase in temperature can be detected through software in the heat detector. The device is usually contained in a white plastic shell which is mounted to the ceiling.

Smoke Detectors

Smoke detectors make use of two sensing methods to detect the presence of smoke: the photoelectric method and the ionization chamber method.

The sensor in a photoelectric detector comprises a light source, usually from infrared LEDs which shine onto a photodiode. When smoke enters the detector, smoke particles begin to obscure the light source and the photodiode senses this and triggers the alarm. Filters can be used to reduce stray infrared noise.

Ionization smoke detectors contain a tiny amount of a radioactive isotope, Americium 241, which emits alpha particles causing ionization of the air within a smoke detector. When smoke enters the detecting chamber of the detector, the ionized air molecules react with the smoke causing a change in the chamber's electrostatic field and triggering the alarm. Like heat detectors, smoke detector devices are usually contained in white plastic shells mounted to the ceiling.

Other sensors are available for specialist applications where the fire load or detection distances are unusual. These include multi-sensor detectors using both photoelectric and heat sensors in combination, carbon monoxide detectors and beam detectors which can be used to detect across large open areas.

Aspirating Detectors

In the retail environment, where a clean, uncluttered ceiling is desired, aspiration detectors can provide an alternative to ceiling-mounted plastic detector heads. Aspirating detectors work by sampling the air throughout the store through small sampling heads connected to a network of capillary and main pipes; these lead to a central smoke detection unit which functions along similar principles to the heads described previously. Because the sampling heads are often no larger than a screw head, they are extremely discreet. This method is often referred to as a VESDA® system, meaning Very Early Smoke Detection System. This name is not, however, generic and is a trademark of Xtralis in the Republic of Ireland.

Audio and Public Address Speakers

The designer has many choices in audio speakers, from flush-mounted recessed speakers to pendants and bracket-mounted cabinet speakers. For very discreet speakers, a hidden speaker mounted into plasterboard is possible. Where speakers are required for public address or life safety the designer faces a more limited choice, particularly where fire-resistant speakers are required.

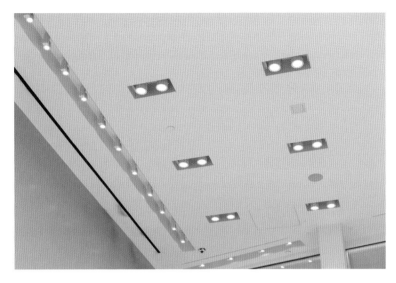

A typically busy retail ceiling at Sugarfina, New York.

Cameras

Cameras are generally installed for the purposes of loss-prevention and security. These range from fixed cameras mounted on brackets to dome cameras, usually ceiling-mounted on a round plate. They will be considered in more detail in the next chapter.

LIGHTING

Whilst the design of the electrical circuits, from which the store's lighting is powered and controlled, falls to the electrical engineer, the lighting design

Well-composed internal and external lighting enhance Gucci at the K11 Art Mall, Hong Kong.

itself is a specialist discipline. Good lighting design plays an enormous role in how the store is perceived by customers, how they see the store's merchandise and what mood is prevalent in the store. We will now explore the types of light fixtures available to the lighting designer and how they can be used.

Lighting Components

The names of lighting components in common parlance differ from those used by lighting designers and engineers and it is important to understand the professionals' vocabulary.

Lamp: the light source, such as a traditional incandescent bulb or, for example, its LED equivalent with a similar socket type

Luminaire: the light fixture into which the lamp or lamps are mounted; this includes all types – suspended, ceiling-mounted or free-standing

Socket: the part of the luminaire that holds the lamp; these are available to receive a number of lamp types such as E14 (screw in), B22 (traditional bayonet), GU10 (twin studs) and so on

LED: light-emitting diode

Driver: a transformer that reduces mains voltage to a low voltage to power LED lamps

Ballast: used with fluorescent and compact fluorescent fittings, the ballast controls the voltage, both to start up the lamp and then regulate voltage when lit

Lamp Types

A lighting designer of the recent past who was specifying projects in the first decade of the millennium could draw on a wide variety of lamp types. These might have included metal halide for ambient lighting and display purposes, perhaps halogen for accent lighting, incandescent for decorative purposes and possibly fluorescent fittings incorporated into display fittings. Each type was well suited to the job in hand, with known colour temperatures, dimming properties and lifespans. Whilst LED was commercially available at the time, the range of lamps was limited but, more crucially, the manufacturing technology was not well enough developed to ensure the stability of colour temperature or the life of the product.

If we look at today's market, we see that enormous strides have been taken with LED design and manufacturing so that this type of lamp is now almost universally used in retail design. At the 2020 Euro-Shop retail trade fair in Düsseldorf, for example, 120 exhibitors presented lighting products and without exception all offered products based on LED technology. Of interest to the retail designer is that the character and variety of lighting created from the traditional palette can now be achieved using LED alone. As is widely known, LED is also more energy-efficient than its predecessors. The US Department of Energy estimates that by 2027 the widespread use of LEDs could save about 348 terawatt-hours (TWh) of electricity. This is the equivalent annual electrical output of forty-four 1,000 megawatt electric power plants, or total savings of more than $30 billion (based on 2020 electricity prices). The LED's energy efficiency also results in less waste heat, reducing the load on cooling systems in the store. For these reasons, the scope of this chapter will be limited to LED as a light source. If other lamp types are encountered in projects where the designer's brief is to modify an existing store, most traditional lamps can now be replaced with LED equivalents designed to fit the existing sockets.

Luminaire Types

The range of luminaires available to the designer has never been wider and care should be taken when specifying. Wherever possible, sample fittings should

be obtained and mock-up installations prepared to verify both
the quality of the luminaire and
illumination produced. Good
mock-ups allow a variety of both
luminaires and lamps to be tested
with actual products and this can
help avoid lighting mistakes in the
final scheme. In the retail environment the key groups of luminaires
are broadly as listed below.

Recessed fittings in combination with a grid of suspended fittings. H&M, Shoppes At Venetian, Macao.

Ceiling-Recessed Luminaires

Commonly referred to as down-
lights, these luminaires sit within
the ceiling void and are usually
mounted flush with the ceiling.
The luminaire is generally secured with spring clips
that clamp against the back of the ceiling plasterboard
with a bezel or trim around the fitting covering the
edge of the aperture in which it is fitted. Trimless luminaires without bezels can be plastered into the ceiling to
produce a neater finish. Whilst ceiling-recessed luminaires can be found with three or more lamps, the more
usual is a single lamp fitting. The fitting can be tailored
to provide the desired light beam by
means of its reflector and lens. Addi-
tionally, the luminaire can incorporate a movable gimbal, allowing
the direction of the light beam to
be adjusted. Whilst the location
of a ceiling-recessed luminaire is
fixed once installed, it is still possible to achieve a variety of effects
from adjacent fittings and so these
fittings could be made to provide
both accent and ambient lighting.

Track-Mounted Luminaires

For flexibility, track-mounted
luminaires offer the most
straightforward solution. The track on which the
luminaires are mounted carries the power at the
required voltage, allowing the luminaires to clip
on using an industry standard such as Eurostand-
ard Plus®. This allows some mixing and matching
between manufacturers of track and manufacturers
of luminaires. The track is generally supplied with
three circuits, although single or double circuits

Track lighting used to give great accenting at Maje, Luxembourg.

may still be found on older installations. When installing the luminaire, the track can be selected allowing various settings such as all luminaires lit (when the store is trading) to only a handful lit (overnight for security purposes). The tracks can be recessed, surface-mounted or hung from cables to suit the desired aesthetic. Track-mounted lighting is flexible because, within reason, the number of luminaires on the track can be increased without recourse to additional wiring or builder's work. Equally, the number of luminaires can be reduced if a change in effect is required. Track-mounted luminaires are usually fitted with gimbals and so specific focussing of lighting on product can be easily set up and adjusted.

LED Strip

LED strip lighting comprises a flexible tape which is actually a circuit board onto which the diodes are mounted. When a low voltage power source is introduced to the circuit, the individual LEDs emit light. The effect can be a series of small white dots, but if the strip is set behind a diffuser, the light is softened and a more uniform appearance is achieved. Advances in LED technology mean that thin flexible tape with equally flexible diffusers are available and LED is now the popular choice for built-in lighting in display furniture, whereas in the past fluorescent lighting, along with its bulky ballasts, would have been used. As well as uses in display furniture, LED strip can be used in niches to create a light-wash effect from a concealed source.

Free-Standing Decorative Luminaires

Whilst playing a limited role in providing a useful light source, decorative luminaires add to the character and ambience of a store. Unfortunately, floor-standing or tabletop luminaires are often introduced into a project with little thought as to how they are installed. Domestic plug and socket arrangements are not usually appropriate as the sockets are easily tampered with by cleaning staff looking for vacuum cleaner power or, worse, curious children who are at risk of electric shock. A better method is to hard-wire decorative fittings to a spur which can be switched or isolated independently.

Chandelier or light sculpture? This fixture adds interest in a mall space enjoying much natural light in the daytime. Dubai Mall, United Arab Emirates.

Pendant Fittings

What we think of as domestic pendant fittings hung from a ceiling rose can be found in the retail environment, particularly where emphasis is required on a particular area of the sales floor. Larger pendant fittings are more often described as chandeliers and these can be used to good effect where the ceiling height allows. Where the ceiling design is open, fittings suspended on cables are strictly to be described as pendant fittings unless mounted on a track.

Understanding Light Quality

Colour Temperature

When the lighting designer specifies a lamp, it is understood to emit white light. This is not, however, the whole story as the range of artificial white light sources can vary just as daylight does. We understand, for example, that the sun's light in the morning or at the end of the day is warmer in colour than, for instance, at midday when the sun is at the highest point in the sky. This is a variation of colour temperature, which should not to be confused with thermal temperature. White light colour temperature is measured in kelvins, with 4,000 kelvin (K) being perceived as a neutral white, neither warm nor cold. A warm colour temperature light source would start from around 2,400K, with 6,500K representing a cold temperature. The importance of colour temperature is that the appearance of the object being illuminated varies according to the colour temperature of the light source. Traditionally, certain foodstuffs have been lit in a specific way to enhance their appearance and appeal to customers; for example, the butcher's counter benefits from being lit with warmer-coloured lighting to enhance the red of the meat. In fashion retail, the product might be lit with a neutral temperature on the shop floor to mimic natural light, with warmer lighting in the fitting rooms to enhance the customer's skin tones when trying on clothes before a mirror. A knowledge of the store's merchandise is therefore a prerequisite for selecting the best colour temperature. LED technology has allowed the development of luminaires with settings that allow the colour temperature to be changed, so that the light emitted can be adjusted to,

Inventive design of trough-type lighting realized as suspended fittings at Aritzia, Hudson Yards, New York.

say, 3,000K, 4,300K or 6,500K. This level of adjustment should not be required in most applications but could provide a useful level of adjustment in enhanced or feature displays.

Brightness

The measure of how much light is produced by a light source is dependent on the temperature of the light because some colours are perceived by the eye as brighter, even if the same amount of light is generated by the source. This subjective measure is called the luminous flux and is quoted by manufacturers as a measure of brightness, measured in lumens. Equally important is to measure how much light is cast on the object being lit or how bright a surface appears. This is measured in lux and one lumen is the light needed to illuminate a square metre of surface with a brightness of one lux. The lux level achieved in different areas of the store is vital to both creating the mood within the store and contributing to how well presented the store's merchandise appears. For example, the store designer may wish to deploy low levels of brightness in walkways between displays, for example 150 lux, but raise this to 1,000 lux to pick out displays of merchandise.

Glare and Reflection

Glare occurs when light sources are so positioned that they interrupt a person's field of vision and are significantly brighter than the background illumination. In simple terms this is avoided by considering the location and direction of light sources and in understanding the extent of our fields of vision. A light source shining on a customer's eyes directly and on the horizontal will cause the maximum glare, but the glare reduces as the angle between the light source and the eyes increases. As a rule, once more than 60 degrees from the horizontal, the light source will not be perceived to cause glare and so the following controls can be used to avoid this potential problem. Most obviously, higher ceilings contribute greatly to

reducing the risk of glare, but where this advantage is not to be had, the design should avoid light source locations that produce shallow beam angles (from the horizontal). This problem most often occurs when luminaires are directed onto merchandise from too far away, possibly because the position of the luminaires is wrong or the merchandising of the store has changed without considering how it is to be lit.

Glare is not only a problem when it originates from the original light source but can also occur through secondary glare from a particularly reflective surface, such as a highly polished black granite floor. As with glare generally, avoiding low beam angles and long throws of light can help avoid this.

Reflection can be a problem where polished surfaces, glass or mirrors create lighting effects that are unintended. Vitrine displays should be designed with this in mind as light sources intended to be concealed can easily be revealed by reflection, thus spoiling the overall effect. Equally, installing large mirrors, and particularly those that reach, or almost reach, ceiling height allow unexpected views into the ceiling which can reveal the workings of otherwise concealed light sources.

Lighting Control

The simplest lighting control is, of course, the on-off switch but the retail environment brief is rarely as simple as that. At its most basic, the store's lighting control system should allow for scene setting or pre-programmed configurations of the lighting. This might include the situation when the store is trading and both ambient and accent lighting is fully deployed. Equally, there will be times when only ambient lighting is required, perhaps for cleaning and maintenance purposes. Finally, there may an unoccupied state where display windows only are lit. More sophisticated control systems, in combination with the appropriate luminaires, can control the dimming of lamps in response to the amount of natural daylight entering the store. Not only does this help to maintain a more consistent level of lighting throughout the course of the day but it also contributes to energy saving. Energy usage monitoring, another facet of a sophisticated control system, allows retailers to understand the cost of their lighting and to make informed choices about adjustments to the lighting scheme.

As we can see, the ability to vary colour temperature and brightness and to control the lighting installation are all key to lighting a store effectively, but so are the purposes to which lighting is deployed.

Lighting Groups

Ambient Lighting

This is the primary source of lighting in the store and, as noted above, is generally provided through ceiling-mounted luminaires. This is the lighting that sets the mood of the store and helps define its character. Well-designed ambient lighting will certainly encourage footfall but it would be a mistake to think that an arms race to ever brighter interiors necessarily leads to more store visitors. Areas of contrasting light and shade, the use of natural light and a careful choice of colour temperature are all equally good strategies to attract customers and to create an appealing environment in which to shop.

Accent Lighting

Within retail lighting design, accent lighting assumes a significance beyond anything seen in other types of interiors. It is rarely sufficient to rely on ambient lighting alone to best display and highlight products, either on the shelf or rail, or to show mannequins and other visual merchandising to best effect. The accent lighting should adjust to reflect seasonal trends and changes in product lines, and so flexibility and the ability to adjust the position and quantity of luminaires is key. As we have seen, track-mounted fittings usually provide the required flexibility. Where product is sold primarily from shelves, overhead light sources can produce shadows over product and this is where accent lighting incorporated into the display furniture can be useful.

Ambient lighting from back-lit panels with accent lighting from track-mounted fittings at Forty Five Ten, Hudson Yards, New York.

The emphasis on accent lighting over ambient or task lighting creates a high contrast between product display and the background spaces. M&G, Beijing.

Whilst this approach focusses attention on the product, it is not without difficulties. Note how much of the outer-facing product is cast in shadow from the shelf above. M&G, Beijing.

Task Lighting

Task lighting illuminates those areas of the store requiring additional light such as the point of sale cash desks or the fitting rooms. Fitting room lighting requires extra consideration, for, as we have seen when discussing colour temperature, the customer should be presented with not only an attractive reflection of themselves but also a well-lit space so that they can see and test the fit of the garment.

Decorative Lighting

The use of decorative fittings has little to do with the practicalities of illuminating the store or its sales surfaces, but rather in creating points of interest in the store. For example, where the store design's theme wishes to convey a relaxed and domestic mood, stand-alone decorative fittings might help in creating a residential ambience. Equally, a brand may wish to place a statement piece such as a chandelier as a focal point on entering the store. Whilst the chandelier may well provide a source of light, no doubt track-mounted gimbal fittings will be doing the work of illuminating the product.

Emergency Light Fittings and Direction Signs

Whilst not a lighting group to which the store designer usually pays much attention, it is worthwhile

Sculptural decorative light fittings at Tom Dixon, Coal Drops Yard, London.

understanding the requirements for emergency lighting and options to incorporate it in the store design. Emergency lighting is provided for use when the supply to the normal lighting fails; in the UK, British Standard BS 5266-1:2016 defines the requirement. Broadly, the minimum level of illuminance required in an escape route is one lux and in open rooms with a floor area of 60m² or more, half of one lux. The standard sets out more detailed criteria than can be covered here, but nevertheless these levels illustrate that, in most cases, achieving this standard should not adversely impact the main lighting systems.

Emergency lighting is either described as maintained or non-maintained. Maintained lighting is lit continuously and will continue to work in the event of a power failure, albeit at a lower level of brightness. Non-maintained lighting is designed to switch on in the event of a power failure. In both cases the back-up power is either supplied by a battery located in the luminaire or from a central battery unit possibly supplying a wider area such as a mall or transport hub. The issue faced by the designer is that whilst a maintained system does not give rise to additional fittings to accommodate in the lighting scheme, not all luminaires can be sourced with emergency light capability and so the choice of luminaires becomes slightly limited. On the other hand, if a non-maintained fitting is specified, it functions independently of the main lighting. The

issue with non-maintained lighting, however, is that for the majority of the time, the fitting is not illuminated and care should be taken to source fittings which do not appear dead or broken when not lit.

Direction signage, more commonly known as 'running man' signage, is required to guide occupants of the store to safe exit points or give direction along an escape route. As with emergency lighting, illuminated direction signs can either be maintained or non-maintained. The default fitting is a light box with the appropriate vinyl indicating direction of escape applied over. Fortunately, more considered designs, often using edge-lit acrylic, are now widely available.

Lighting Scheme Design

The lighting designer's concept should develop hand-in-hand with the store design concept, so integral is it to the success of the scheme. Concept designs might include plan drawings showing the layout of luminaires, 3D images showing the intended lighting effect, or both methods. Lighting calculations are then made to check that the desired lighting levels are achieved, ideally based on a shared model of the project, with an accurate representation of the finishes and materials. As the design develops,

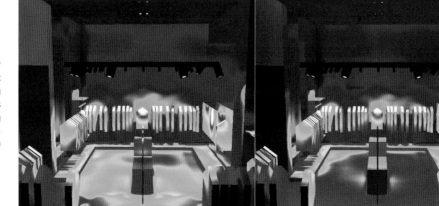

Computer modelling of light levels showing daytime settings (L) and evening settings (R). (Photo: giaEquation)

the selection of luminaires and lamps can be made. Ideally, a test model can be populated with luminaires and thus, using photometric data from the luminaire manufacturers, photo-realistic models of the interior and the lighting effect can be generated. The same data set can be used to verify lux levels over the retail floor, the effectiveness of beam angles or to indicate where there might be a risk of glare.

As noted previously, mock-ups of key parts of the interior such as ceilings and display furniture can be of enormous benefit in testing that the concept works as anticipated. Whilst funding the cost of a mock-up and finding the space in which to construct it can be challenging, the learning to be gained from mock-ups cannot be overstated. Where display furniture, floor finishes or other key elements of the interior are being sampled or mocked-up, it is beneficial to be able to see these under the same lighting conditions that are envisaged for the final scheme. This is therefore an ideal time to test luminaire options and finalize the specification.

Once the selection has been finalized, drawings of the lighting layout are produced, along with a specification for the luminaires and lamps. Where the lighting control requires separate circuits or scenes, these should be indicated on the drawing so that the wiring can be installed to suit. Once the lighting is installed on site, the system is commissioned to ensure that the controls perform as intended. Just as important is the 'focussing' of the luminaires, particularly gimbal fittings on tracks, which must be located in the correct position and directed to achieve the best effect. This is often undertaken with the store's merchandising team who will have a view on what they wish to be lit and how it is achieved.

Lighting and Architectural Details

As we have seen, the store's ceiling can be crowded with other services, thus requiring careful coordination of the lighting. The lighting design is often integral to the success of architectural details, particularly where the ceiling is concerned.

Troughs

Ceiling troughs are useful because they allow light sources to be completely or partially concealed, allowing a much neater appearance to the ceiling. There are a variety of trough designs, each suiting a different method of lighting.

Whilst it might be tempting the keep the trough opening narrow, the geometry of the trough must allow for the luminaire's beam to be uninterrupted by the vertical faces of the trough. The track position and the size of the luminaire both contribute to this calculation, as does an understanding of the proposed beam positions. It may be that the design requires all luminaires to sit wholly within the trough whereas at other times the design encourages the ends of the luminaires to sit slightly below the ceiling plane.

Where a trough is constructed with a slot, this geometry becomes more complicated still and, in addition, sufficient space must be allowed for the access which will be required to locate luminaires on the track, positioning and focussing and then for future re-lamping and maintenance.

Coves, Coffers and Rafts

Coves are often used to create a wash or glow around the perimeter of the room. A similar effect is created with ceiling rafts and coves and all rely on a concealed light source, usually LED strip. As with the design of troughs, geometry is critical to avoid creating harsh shadows from the edge behind which the light source sits. A sense check should be made that the LED strip remains concealed, particularly when seen from unusual angles or heights such as a staircase or escalator.

Ceiling Reinforcement

In most cases, the standard methods of construction of ceilings, bulkheads and troughs will provide adequate support for lighting systems. The exception might be where a single point-load is applied to

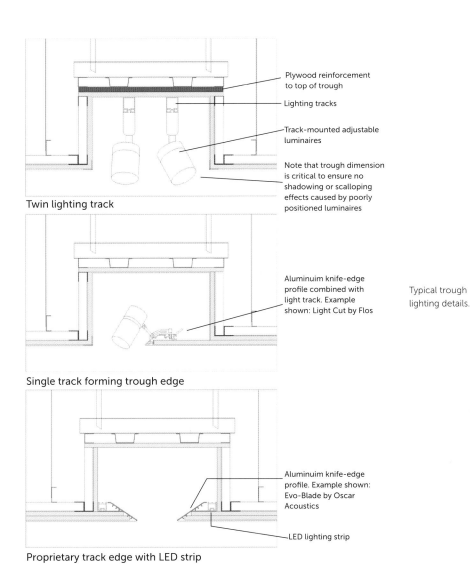

Twin lighting track

Plywood reinforcement
to top of trough

Lighting tracks

Track-mounted adjustable
luminaires

Note that trough dimension
is critical to ensure no
shadowing or scalloping
effects caused by poorly
positioned luminaires

Single track forming trough edge

Aluminuim knife-edge
profile combined with
light track. Example
shown: Light Cut by Flos

Typical trough
lighting details.

Proprietary track edge with LED strip

Aluminuim knife-edge
profile. Example shown:
Evo-Blade by Oscar
Acoustics

LED lighting strip

Track lighting in
a ceiling trough
at Burberry,
Selfridges, London.
(Photo: Hyphen)

the ceiling, for instance in the installation of a large pendant or a chandelier fitting. In this case the additional load should be taken up with a substructure, independent of the plasterboard ceiling framing and anchored to the soffit or structural beam. For smaller loads requiring more robust support, a plywood pattress can be incorporated into the ceiling, to which mechanical fixings can be made.

Fixture Lighting

As discussed above, placing the light source solely in the ceiling may create problems of overshadowing, particularly with shelving. This can be overcome through shelf lighting, usually an LED strip run along the back of the shelf edge.

This solution works best when the product on display sits some distance below or back from the shelf edge. Shelves that are merchandised as pigeonholes full of product probably benefit little from this and are best lit from above, but this should be from multiple light sources to prevent overshadowing by the customer as they browse.

The lighting of glass vitrines requires a careful approach as the type of product usually displayed within is generally of greater value and higher price point, such as watches and jewellery. The lighting should be designed to allow the product to sparkle and so bright, focussed light is required. LED luminaires can be designed to be extremely small and so good options to consider could be corner posts or strips incorporating miniature fittings with a variety of possible beam widths to provide the best focus on products. In one sense the display vitrine should be considered as the retail space in miniature, with the same design considerations going to providing ambient and accent lighting. Even though LED lighting does not generate the waste heat of its halogen equivalent, consideration should be given to ventilating vitrines to avoid excessive temperature gain.

Illuminated Display

Illuminated display, both as a light source and as a means of enhancing the display of product, can

Subtle LED lighting incorporated into the shelf edge at Forty Five Ten, Hudson Yards, New York.

LED vertical strip and micro spotlights emphasize the sparkle in this jewellery vitrine. Bulgari, Heathrow Airport Terminal 3, London.

Simple yet effective display using retro-looking fluorescent tube fittings to emphasize the colour and form of the product at Nike House of Innovation, New York.

create an arresting and interesting counterpoint to traditional shelving. Because solid objects on an illuminated background will appear darker in contrast, this method lends itself to transparent or semi-transparent objects such as glassware or eyewear. As the light source is from behind or below the object being lit, a secondary light source directed at the product face is also required.

CASE STUDY: LUSH LIVERPOOL

Lush's largest anchor store opened in 2019 and comprises two floors of retail, a spa, a hair salon and a coffee corner. The store's size of over 1,380m² public space, with its extensive display windows and high ceilings, conveys the mood of a concept store or a small department store. This is deliberate and reflects the influence of the existing building on the development of the design. The building was purpose-built by Woolworth to designs by their in-house architect William Priddle, opening in 1923. Woolworth had actually developed the larger building block in which Lush now sits, located on the northern boundary of the Liverpool One development. At the time of the opening, Montague Burton and C&A Modes were tenants of Woolworth with their own substantial stores. Prior to Lush taking possession of the site it had been occupied and much altered by the Arcadia Group; in the 1990s they had enclosed or blocked up the original display windows and installed escalators. The Arcadia Group design for their Topshop and Topman brands did little to recognize the character and quality of William Priddle's original design.

Main entrance to Lush Liverpool anchor store. The original rhythm of display windows has been reinstated in the restored façade. (Photo: Lush)

Lush recognized Liverpool as a great city for retail, having had a presence there for many years prior to the new store opening. Liverpool was also seen as an ideal market in which to include a spa as part of the store's offer. Whilst the spa is not unique to the Liverpool store, no other Lush store had attempted anything as large before.

Lush, supported by architects Hyphen, set about discovering the 'bones' of the original building which archive photos demonstrated to have been a characteristically practical yet elegant inter-war design. The escalators were removed, allowing the original floor plates to be reinstated, including a fine original atrium offering an immediate visual connection between the ground and first floors and creating a strong impression of height and volume on the main retail floor. The existing ground-floor levels were rationalized and lifts refurbished, allowing for barrier-free access to the store. The late twentieth-century storefront was removed and the ground-floor façade was remodelled with new Portland stone columns and new display windows reflecting the original 1920s design. Lush had considered installing a new staircase to draw customers to the upper floors but this idea proved impractical and so it was decided to utilize the original staircase which had originally enclosed the goods lift. This staircase had been stripped of its balustrades by the previous occupants and adjustments were required to suit the new floor levels. The goods lift was relocated to allow the staircase to be incorporated into the store's new design and it became one of the store's most interesting and attractive architectural features.

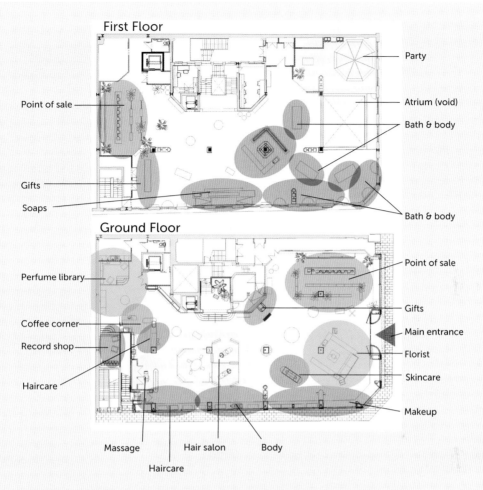

First Floor

Point of sale

Gifts

Soaps

Party

Atrium (void)

Bath & body

Bath & body

Ground Floor

Perfume library

Coffee corner

Record shop

Haircare

Point of sale

Gifts

Main entrance

Florist

Skincare

Makeup

Massage   Hair salon   Body

Haircare

Plans for ground and first floors showing main product groupings. (Photo: Hyphen)

View across ground floor showing the coffered ceiling derived from the building's original downstand beams; against this structure, the fixtures are arranged informally. (Photo: Lush)

The original Woolworth interior comprised high, open ceilings, bright white walls and dark mahogany display furniture and counters. Whilst the original fit-out has long been removed, the Lush design sought to capture this aesthetic, adapting it to the needs of a contemporary store. The ceiling retains the pattern of beams and soffits, with new air-conditioning ductwork and lighting carefully incorporated.

The customer experience is central to Lush's success, with product demonstrations, a hair salon and the extensive spa facilities. The grandeur of the original building and the space it affords allow the

Atrium between the ground and first floors allowing a visual connection between different product groups. (Photo: Lush)

Free-standing skincare display; natural light floods the retail spaces, with minimal emphasis on artificial lighting. (Photo: Lush)

Point of sale area demarcated using a solid block of black on the rear wall. (Photo: Lush)

The point of sale is designed with a nod to the original Woolworth perimeter display of the inter-war years. (Photo: Lush)

More formal display units in the perfume library area. (Photo: Lush)

Dark wood wall panelling emphasizes the top of the fixture zone, allowing the elegant white ceiling to float above. (Photo: Lush)

customer the freedom to explore the retail floors, led as much by the vibrant displays and the fragrances of the product as by a designer's pre-determined route through the store. Supporting this are product demonstrations that remain key to Lush's relationship with its customers. The building services are designed to ensure that hot water is available where needed and this attention to detail ensures that both hard and soft water is available for hair washing as different hair types benefit from different levels of hardness.

To create the right ambience, the spa rooms are soundproofed and the lighting is programmed to vary throughout the customer's stay and in response to their treatment. Lush's philosophy is to have the product stand out on its own merits and so the display furniture is modest and deliberately intended to offer a quiet, simple backdrop to the products on sale.

The store's offer is wide and includes a coffee corner and a record shop. (Photo: Lush)

Natural light and real indoor plants are put to good use in the hair salon. (Photo: Lush)

Carefully designed fixtures allow for generous merchandising. (Photo: Lush)

View across first floor with elegant tiered displays. (Photo: Lush)

Since Lush was founded in Poole, Dorset, in 1995 it has operated with a strong commitment to sustainability and fair trade. This ethos informed the specification of materials and finishes and so the store includes re-purposed and recycled materials, as well as new materials selected for their environmentally responsible credentials. Whereas the 1920s architect could specify tropical hardwoods, this is no longer possible and so to create the dark wood of the original, stained veneers are used instead.

The overall impression is of a contemporary redux of inter-war department store: modern and of our time but respectfully and comfortably inhabiting William Priddle's original structure.

The entry to the spa reflects the aesthetic of the retail floors. (Photo: Lush)

Sound and light are carefully controlled in the spa treatment rooms. (Photo: Lush)

Rolling racking at Lush Liverpool. (Photo: Lush)

Chapter Eight

Store Operations

I N RETAIL, 'BACK OF HOUSE' REFERS TO THE store's functions that are out of sight to the shopper but nevertheless essential to the successful management of a store. Retailers will naturally wish to maximize their selling space but it is essential to the success of the store that the back of house space is well designed to allow the store to function efficiently.

BACK OF HOUSE ORGANIZATION

Stockroom

The stockroom is where the merchandise not on the shop floor is stored. The stockroom size is determined by the range of stock-keeping units (SKUs), the physical size required to store them and the rate of sales and replenishment. For example, a shoe shop may display a number of different styles in the store but will carry a range of sizes, thus leading to multiple

SKUs. The stockroom in this case is likely to be frequently accessed as part of the sales process and thus demands a stock area that can be quickly accessed by sales staff and be easily navigated. Where a high percentage of the store's merchandise is on display on the shop floor, the stockroom is accessed less frequently as part of the sales process and a less efficient arrangement can perhaps be forgiven.

Stockroom Space Planning

Whilst there is no definitive rule for calculating the ratio between the sales area and the back of house area, a good rule of thumb as a starting point in most stores is 65 per cent sales area and 35 per cent back of house. In this case, the sales area includes display windows, fitting rooms, private sales rooms, consultation rooms and public staircases. The back of house area includes the stockroom, staff welfare, offices and any non-public circulation areas. The stockroom area will vary according to the product in stock but, again

A well-managed stockroom at Lush Liverpool. (Photo: Hyphen)

by rule of thumb, an area of around 15 per cent of the total is considered fairly standard. It should be stressed that the above ratios serve as no more than initial guidance, but are nevertheless derived from surveying a vast pool of stores of varying sizes selling a wide variety of product. From the starting point of 65 per cent sales, 15 per cent stock and 20 per cent miscellaneous back of house functions, we can see how the type of retail, the store's location and its size all influence these ratios.

Stockroom Areas

The ratio of stockroom area to sales floor area varies according to the nature of the business. Where the store sits within a single-storey, rectangular white box, such as a mall store, our rule of thumb is fairly applicable, although some mall operators offer remote stockroom space which allows a higher proportion of sales area in the mall unit. Nevertheless, mall stores tend towards a high degree of efficiency, with external public toilets and landlord plantrooms removed from the retailer's demise.

The same efficiency can be achieved for stand-alone stores in retail parks, where there are few or no constraints to the internal space planning. Where the store is located in an airport or as a shop-in-shop in a department store, the stockroom tends not to occupy valuable retail space and so remote stockrooms or cages are provided to support the retail operation. In this case, the ratio between sales and back of house can appear very high.

High street sites can be fairly efficient but in cases where the building has an unusual footprint or multiple floors, we tend to see the efficiency declining. It can be difficult to encourage shoppers to visit upper floors in a multi-storey store, which tends to give rise to the allocation of entire upper floors to non-sales functions. In addition, back of house staircases, goods lifts and multiple stockrooms serving different floors all use space allocation.

As well as the building type and location, the nature of retail operation itself will have a large impact on the back of house area, including the stockroom size. For example, a trade-counter store will typically trade from only a very small sales floor displaying no

Percentage of Gross Internal Floor Area allocated to stockroom	Example Retail Type	Commentary
0% to 2%	Watches & Jewellery	Small items usually secured in safe of strong room
2% to 5%	Optical	High percentage of stock held in shop floor in display cupboards
2% to 10%	Apparel	Fast fashion brands with high turnover requiring less stock to be held off the sales floor
10% to 15%	Electrical & Technology	High value and relative small size requires secure stock room
10% to 20%	Shoes & Accessories	Varies according to SKU count and to accommodate seasonal variation
15% to 20%	Grocery	Varies according to the requirements for chilled storage
20% to 25%	Designer Fashion	Typically fewer pieces displayed on the sales floor
75% to 90%	Trade Counters	Generally building materials, electrical, plumbing or parts

Typical stockroom area ratios according to type of retail.

more than a tiny fraction of the store's inventory. The sales operation may be supported through catalogues or be the click and collect function of an omnichannel approach to retailing.

Garment and shoe retailing demands that the store carries a range of sizes and it is here that we see the stock area allocation most often adhering to the rule of thumb. A note of caution should be sounded over shoe stockrooms, however, as this is an area where the stockroom's efficiency and location has a direct bearing on the sales staff's ability to serve the customer. For example, a shoe store with men's, women's and children's shoe departments spread over different floors can ill afford to rely on a single stockroom as the travel distances and the time required to bring shoes to customers would be too long, invariably leading to a loss of sales. Shoe fashions and seasonal trends have a direct impact on the stockroom capacity; for example, the box space occupied by a pair of long boots in the winter might be three or four times the volume of a box containing pumps in the summer.

At the opposite end of the scale are those retailers selling small, precious goods, typically watches and jewellery, who may not be required to carry multiple SKUs and who expect stock to be stored in a secure safe or vault.

A recent retail phenomenon has been the rise of fashion-led opticians, often offering a fast-fashion approach to the fitting and supply of eyewear. The store itself may display only try-on pairs, with the production facility located remotely, or it may opt to carry stock within the retail display furniture. This arrangement can result in stores with very little apparent stock area.

Stock Control

Within the stockroom itself is a small area, perhaps as small as a work table or bench, where incoming merchandise is unpacked, entered into the store's inventory and placed either on the shop floor or into the stockroom.

Racking

The stockroom racking should be selected to suit the store's merchandise and will usually comprise shelving or hanging rails storage. Where capacity is limited, it may be worthwhile considering mobile storage or rolling racking.

The use of rolling racking can double the storage capacity available in comparison to fixed shelving. This type of shelving requires floor tracks, either recessed in the floor or more typically surface-mounted. The shelf bays move along these tracks, usually by means of a hand-turned wheel at the end of the shelf. Unless the stock is particularly heavy, a light-grade rack which can accommodate most retail stock to a height of around 2.4m is suitable. Higher racking is possible, but unless there is a necessity to install this, it can become a hazard for staff who have to use stepladders to reach higher shelves. Not only can this create risks to health and safety but retrieving and relocating stepladders can slow down the locating

A busy back-office desk from which to process incoming stock and manage the store.

and retrieval of stock. With the more standard height racking, a wheeled step-stool (or so-called 'elephant foot' stool) is usually the only aid required. When planning rolling racking, the shelf bays are usually accessed from both sides, typically with an overall depth of between 800mm and 1200mm. When planning rolling racking, the end bays are usually fixed half bays and the rolling bays are set out to leave a working aisle of around 1000 mm.

Staff Welfare

The facilities provided vary from store to store according to the type of store, its size and the statutory requirements in force. In some cases, such as in shopping malls or department stores, staff welfare (that is to say, locker rooms, toilets, rest areas and canteens) are located centrally and the individual operators do not concern themselves with providing stand-alone facilities. Generally, however, room for staff welfare must be found in the back of house area where there is already competition for space. It is therefore rare that welfare facilities ever have the luxury of being oversized. The first two things to understand when planning facilities are the staffing levels and the statutory requirements in force. The total number of staff employed in the store is unlikely to be the critical factor in space planning. More usefully the design can be based on the peak capacity of staff, which will vary according to shift patterns and increased staffing at busy sales periods. In the largest stores, peak shift numbers could be considerable, necessitating dedicated changing, showering facilities and locker rooms. In addition, nursing mothers'

rooms, a first aid room or a union representative office may all be required. Let us assume, though, that we are considering a typical high street store where only a few staff are employed in a regular shift pattern. In the UK, the Health and Safety at Work Act 1974 contains various regulations designed to protect the well-being of people in the workplace. The scope of the act is wide but there are several standards relevant to the design and operation of a store.

HSE Workplace (Health, Safety and Welfare) Regulations on washing facilities require that sufficient toilet and washing facilities are provided to allow everyone at work to use them without unreasonable delay. If the facilities are located remotely, staff should not have to walk more than 100m or travel up or down more than one floor to use them. The number of WCs and wash basins required is set out in the table below.

These numbers are based on shared facilities and if facilities are allocated by gender, a separate calculation must be made for both male and female groups. Where toilets are provided for a large number of male staff, it is possible to reduce the number of WCs through the provision of urinals. However, other than department stores employing several hundred people, this is unlikely to be a consideration in smaller stores.

As well as able-bodied facilities, there should be suitable toilets designed for wheelchair users and ambulant disabled people. Because a WC that is suitable for wheelchair users also serves able-bodied staff, it is possible, for example, to accommodate a maximum shift of twenty-five staff, with one WC designed for wheelchair use and one for able-bodied use, provided both are unisex.

HSE Workplace (Health, Safety and Welfare) Regulations also state that a changing room should

Number of people at work	Number of WCs	Number of washbasins
1 to 5	1	1
6 to 25	2	2
26 to 50	3	3

Toilet provision for back of house areas.

be provided for staff who change into special work clothing, defined by the Regulations as 'clothing that is only worn at work, such as overalls, uniforms, thermal clothing and hats worn for food hygiene purposes', and it notes that separate changing rooms for male and female staff may be required for reasons of propriety. Unless, however, these specific conditions are present, it might be possible to offer limited changing facilities within the WC cubicle or alongside staff lockers. Wherever staff change, a well-lit mirror should be provided so that staff can check their personal grooming before entering the sales area.

It is particularly important to provide suitable seating at break periods for sales staff who generally stand to carry out their work on the sales floor. As well as adequate seating, the break room should be equipped with facilities for making hot drinks, a refrigerator and a sink with hot and cold (drinking) water. The small store's break room will inevitably be used for staff briefings and announcements. Generous noticeboards should be provided on which to post information on shift rosters, sales results and targets and updates on new products, sales campaigns and in-store events.

Staff Lockers

Locker sizes vary and are designed to store a wide variety of personal items, ranging from motorcycle helmets to long winter coats. When planning lockers, selecting a block with a variety of door sizes allows some flexibility amongst users. Like the rest of the back of house, the lockers are subjected to high wear and hard use and so a robust locker design is required.

Back of House Operations

Waste Management

In the UK, the Environmental Protection Act 1990 places a duty on a store's management to responsibly dispose of the waste produced by the business. The sorting and disposal of waste can represent a significant cost to the store, both in pure cost terms and in the space needed to undertake this. The retail sector handles wide ranges of products, most of which generate packaging waste, to which might be added food waste or damaged stock waste. Packaging waste is primarily paper and cardboard but can also contain plastics, wooden pallets and metal pallet straps. Customers look to brands to operate as sustainably as possible and so stores should be designed to allow for the recycling of waste materials, particularly those that are known to arrive regularly and with each delivery of stock. Space for a number of sorting bins should be provided, either in the loading and unloading area or possibly in a remote location if the store is located in a mall. The number of bins, their size and the type of waste material they receive should reflect the store's needs but this is also influenced by the frequency of collection by either a commercial waste disposal company or a municipal authority. Smaller bins may therefore be adequate when collection times are more frequent. Commercial bins range in volume from 240 litres to over 1,000 litres.

In cases where a large store must dispose of large volumes of cardboard waste, balers can considerably reduce volumes of cartons and boxes down to dense bales. Modern cardboard balers can be located inside the receiving area or outside the store, allowing some flexibility in space planning.

Back of House Management

Ideally, the store manager should be provided with an office from which to administer the store away from the noise and distraction of the selling space. In smaller stores, space for a separate office may not be available and it is not unknown for the management of a store to be transacted from as little as a laptop permanently set up on a shelf or worktop in the stockroom.

Where space permits for a separate office, thought should be given to planning it to accommodate not only a work station and a suitable chair but also lockable file storage, a safe and CCTV monitoring equipment.

IT Rack Space

Stores are increasingly dependent on technology to function as intended, not only in terms of customer sales transactions but also inventory control, asset tagging, security, customer behaviour monitoring and music and audio feeds. The store's IT rack is therefore now an essential back of house feature that demands careful planning. Identifying a rack location early in the project allows the wiring infrastructure and any additional cooling to be planned in good time. The industry standard is the 19-inch (482mm) rack and most commercial hardware is designed to sit within this frame dimension. The footprint of this rack type is 800mm wide with a variable depth, usually of between 600mm and 1,000 mm. The rack can be supplied as a cabinet with a lockable door or wall-mounted in a dedicated cupboard. In both cases care should be taken to ensure that additional cooling is provided in cases where the rack equipment generates significant additional heat load.

Other Back of House Considerations

The cramped back of house space, overflowing with newly arrived stock and packaging materials and scarred from heavy use, can often present a stark contrast to the beautifully curated sales area. Store designers should therefore consider what is revealed when doors between front of house and back of house are opened. One useful technique to help soften the transition between the two areas is to ensure that the back of house area finishes and lighting are similar to those experienced by the customer. Once the transition is passed, the finishes should be as robust as possible with walls, and particularly external corners, protected with metal or PVC guards. Lighting can be more functional than in the store and should be maintained at a minimum of 300 lux with no areas between racking left in shadow. For this reason, the arrangement of luminaires should generally reflect the direction and arrangement of racking bays.

SECURITY

Store security encompasses a number of measures that stores take to reduce stock loss and to ensure the physical safety of their staff and customers. These include physical security as well as operational and design considerations.

Store Planning

The layout of the store can have a significant bearing on the opportunity for shoplifting. Professor Ronald Clarke uses the acronym CRAVED to describe the attributes of goods that tend to be stolen from stores. CRAVED refers to Concealable, Removable, Available, Valuable, Enjoyable and Disposable. Where CRAVED items are sold, they are more vulnerable to being stolen when not under the natural surveillance of store staff. High mid-floor displays that block sight lines, corners of the store that are not overlooked and placing CRAVED items next to the exit can all contribute to increasing the opportunities for shoplifters. In small stores which might be operated by just one or two sales staff, good sight lines from the till are an important consideration of the store's internal planning.

Physical Security

Often the standard of physical security is that set by the store's insurers. Their requirements are likely to include the use of particular deadlocks to external doors and measures to protect back of house windows, skylights and other vulnerable access points. In addition to the common requirements for commercial insurance, retailers face the challenge of physically protecting their storefront from theft or vandalism-motivated attack.

The standards that have been developed to assess storefront glazing, in so far as its resistance to attack is concerned, use various test methods which look at different properties of the glass. It is important to understand how these standards differ so that insurers' requirements can be met, particularly for watch and jewellery stores which require a high resistance to attack.

Loss Prevention Standard 1175, issue 8.0, issued by the Loss Prevention Certification Board, is used to assess a wide array of building products including hinges, locks, shutters and storefront glazing. Products are tested against two criteria: the threat level corresponding to the tools used by the intruder and the delay period in minutes offered by the resistance of the material or product. The threat level is stated as a letter (A–H) and the delay as the number of minutes. By way of example, category A tools are small hand tools, such as knives or pliers, whereas category F tools include grinders and sledgehammers. Therefore security rating F5 would apply to a product resisting attack by sledgehammer for five minutes.

Loss Prevention Standard 1270, issue 1.1, refers specifically to the testing of intruder-resistant glazing and classifies glazing according to how resistant it is to local penetration of three varying hole sizes, from a small hole through which a wire could be passed to a hole large enough for hand access, to an opening large enough to allow an intruder to gain access. The tool category required and the time taken to make each penetration produces a grade of between 1 and 8, with the higher number representing the greater resistance. The security rating is the three grades expressed as a three digit number, for example 1.1.2.

As the Loss Prevention Standard makes clear, however, the tests are carried out on material samples and the security rating does not indicate the resistance of the glazing's installation; for instance if the glazing collapses because the frame loses integrity.

European Standard BS EN 356:2000 covers the resistance of glass to manual attack. The standard is based on a mechanical test, either comprising the dropping of a steel sphere on less resistant glass or with a mechanically operated hammer and axe for more resistant glass. The glazing must resist the creation of a 400mm-square hole when subjected to hammer or axe strikes. Security rating P6B achieves up to 50 strikes, P7B up to 70 strikes and P8B over 70 strikes.

Toughened Glass and Laminated Glass

Toughened or tempered glass gets its strength during the manufacturing process from being subjected to intense heat followed by rapid cooling. Whilst toughened glass has resistance to breakage and attack, once broken it fragments into hundreds of tiny pieces so that the storefront is completely breached.

Laminated glazing comprises sheets of glass with a clear interlayer of polyvinyl butyral (PVB) or ethylene-vinyl acetate (EVA). Even when the glass is broken, the interlayer holds the glass in place, allowing the glazing to retain some integrity even when a hole is formed through attack. Because of constraints imposed by the manufacturing process, site cutting is not possible and so laminated glass is usually ordered pre-cut from drawings or site templates. Curved laminated glass can be difficult and expensive to achieve although the use of resin which is poured between two glass sheets and cured with ultraviolet light does make it possible.

When designing storefronts or display windows, and particularly where high-value product is on display, the store designer must establish early on with the retailer and their insurer their expectations for security and their brief for resistance to attack and break-in. Having done so, the constraints on glass size, weight and shape need to be established. Take, for example, a typical refurbishment project. The laminated glass which is designed to a higher security rating could weigh twice that of the traditional annealed glass it is replacing and so upgrades to the frames and façade structure could be required. Where the risk of attack is believed to be mainly an out-of-hours threat, it may be that toughened glass is adequate, with physical protection provided by security shutters.

Ram-Raid Protection

Ram-raiding in London's luxury shopping streets has obtained a lot of publicity in recent years, both for the violence of the act and the damage left in its wake. These stores are particularly vulnerable for a number of reasons, but particularly that they occupy historic buildings, many with protected storefronts that cannot be modified or easily made more secure. Shops that lie adjacent to pedestrian walkways or pavements with dropped kerbs offer little resistance to vehicles driven at speed, and this type of streetscaping is becoming ever more common in our historic cities.

Where the risk of ram-raiding exists and modifications are permitted, the store designer should consider raising and strengthening the stallriser to create a barrier against vehicle impact. If a security shutter is thought necessary to deter ram-raiders, this should be specified with a suitable IWA 14 impact test rating: this is the standard for measuring vehicle impact. In some cases, city centre management organizations can assist retailers whose stores might be vulnerable from ram-raids by allowing the installation of bollards or street furniture designed to obstruct a vehicle's path to the storefront.

CCTV

According to a 2019 study by research website Comparitech, eight of the world's top ten most surveilled cities are in China, with Atlanta and London completing the list. In London 68.4 cameras can be found for every 1,000 people and there appears to be an acceptance that being monitored by CCTV is a part of our daily lives. However, as systems become more complex and automated, surveillance systems have the potential to intrude to a significant degree on people's privacy. Before embarking on the design and installation of a CCTV system, it is important that the retailer understands the current legislation and codes of practice that have been developed to try and strike the correct balance between the rights of the individual and those of system operators. These include the Data Protection Act 2018 and the Home Office guidance document, the Surveillance Camera Code of Practice 2013.

The store's CCTV system is usually intended to act as a deterrent against theft, collect evidence in the event of theft or provide a record in the event of a dispute or incident. Other purposes include door

Effective if unattractive anti-ram raid protection on Briggate, Leeds.

monitoring or to support crowd control and public safety. The store's CCTV system is also increasingly being used to track people movements and analyse customer behaviour for commercial, rather than security, reasons. Two systems of CCTV are possible, analogue and Internet Protocol (IP), and both have their advantages. It is important to understand which system best suits the retailer so that suitable infrastructure to support the chosen system is designed from the outset.

Analogue CCTV

This is the older of the two technologies and relies on cameras that are hard-wired to a digital video recorder (DVR) using either coax, CAT5e or CAT6 ethernet cable. The cable linking each camera feeds the video signal to the DVR as well as providing low voltage power to the camera. Current systems allow high-definition (HD) cameras as well as remote monitoring over the Internet. The disadvantage of an analogue system is that if a new camera is required, or a camera needs to be relocated, this can only be done with works to the cabling. Running new cables or moving existing ones can be disruptive to the store's operations. The advantage of an analogue system is that increasing the number of cameras or the resolution of the video feed places no additional load on the store's network.

IP CCTV

In this system, cameras are connected across the store's network to a router and a network video recorder (NVR), although some IP systems can operate in a decentralized manner as the cameras are able to record directly to remote or cloud-based data storage. Each camera is assigned an internal IP address on the network but the network's capacity is finite and so increasing the number of cameras may limit the resolution or the system's ability to capture video at an adequate frame rate. IP cameras require a low voltage power supply and so, as with analogue cameras, cables must be run to the camera locations.

Some models are, however, designed to mount on three-circuit light track, giving the opportunity to adjust camera positions with ease. For temporary applications, battery-powered cameras are also available. IP CCTV has two significant disadvantages compared to analogue: firstly, a loss of either power or data results in the CCTV failing, and secondly, data protection risks are greater because system access security is more easily breached.

CCTV Cameras

Cameras should be specified with an understanding of their location and what it is they are expected to monitor and record. The issues to consider are the field of view, the lighting conditions and image resolution. For example, a camera that monitors customer flow is likely to require a wide field of view whereas cameras aimed at points of sale or on specific areas of merchandise will require a narrower field.

Bullet Cameras

Small bullet cameras can be mounted discreetly or larger models placed so as to provide a visual deterrent. Generally these cameras use a fixed lens, although varifocal models allow the camera's field of view to be adjusted.

Dome Cameras

The camera is usually fixed but enclosed in a black plastic dome which conceals the direction in which the camera is pointing. A variation on this design is the open-faced dome in which the camera lens is revealed.

PTZ Cameras

'PTZ' refers to pan, tilt and zoom, and this function is made possible by motors in the camera that allow remote controlled movement. Whilst such versatility sounds useful, unless the store has the resource for a full-time camera operator, these functions are unlikely to be put to use in most retail environments.

Asset Protection

Electronic Article Surveillance (EAS)

In simple terms, EAS is the tagging of merchandise often favoured over other loss prevention methods because tagged products remain on display and are therefore accessible to staff and customers. The system usually comprises detector gates with radio antennae that identify electronic tags when these are in close proximity. More discreet systems might use detectors embedded in the floor or ceiling at the store's entrance, or a combination of these plus gates. Hard tags are removed from the merchandise at the point of sale and reused, whereas smaller soft tags are deactivated at the point of sale and can then be disposed of.

Acousto-Magnetic (AM)

AM systems work at low frequency, use a relatively simple detection technology and are difficult for thieves to bypass or block. AM systems use a narrow frequency band which is less likely to be interrupted by spurious signals and is capable of covering relatively large areas. Whilst AM systems are robust, they are only capable of detecting the tag and cannot detect or transmit any further information. Tags are generally removed and reused.

Radio-Frequency (RF)

RF systems work at higher frequencies than AM with a much wider frequency band but are more susceptible to electronic and metallic interference. The advantage to the retailer is that the tagging can be applied through flat or printed-on labels which are deactivated at the point of sale. Standard RF systems are only capable of detecting the tag but as the use of

RFID technology (see below) becomes more widespread, some RF systems can be upgraded.

Radio-Frequency Identification (RFID)

This system operates at an ultra-high frequency, approximately one hundred times that of RF. Unlike AM and RF systems, RFID is a communications technology that allows the transmission of data from the tag to the RFID reader. This means that the tag is no longer used solely for the purposes of combatting theft but can also play a role in product authentication, assisting supply chain management and inventory control. RFID systems can detect tags from longer distances and so the potential for interference and nuisance reads is greater, which might necessitate introducing a merchandise-free zone around the store's exit; this is unlikely to be viable in smaller stores.

POINT OF SALE

The point of sale (POS) is where the sales transaction between the customer and the store takes place. Whilst today's POS equipment is fairly discreet, it owes its existence to the bulky mechanical cash register patented in the US by Ritty and Birch in 1883. The cash register's purpose was to allow the cash from sales to be stored in a secure drawer whilst sales were rung up and tallied so that when the day's trade had finished the cash in the drawer could be checked against the sales recorded. After purchasing the patent, the National Cash Register Company improved the design further, adding a paper tape that recorded individual sales. The POS of today still shares all of the cash register's functions but the metal buttons that rang up sales are now often replaced with a touch screen and the paper tape record of sales is replaced with a digital record. The cash drawer remains but, in the rapidly approaching cashless age, for how much longer?

Cash Desks

Single, all-in-one cash tills are widely used by small businesses and are ideal where little functionality is required. These are tabletop-standing and require little coordination with display furniture. Some models also have scanners, receipt printers and card readers.

More typically, and where retailers demand more from their POS, the system is assembled from separate components that are neatly incorporated into a millwork carcass. It is important to understand the brand's requirements and their equipment specification to ensure that this is well coordinated. The POS system comprises a monitor and a customer display along with a cash drawer, a receipt printer and a computer processor. To this might be added a barcode reader, a card reader and a tag-removing device or label deactivator. In larger, more robust systems, the devices might be networked and supplied with back-up power to ensure that no transaction data is lost in the event of a power failure.

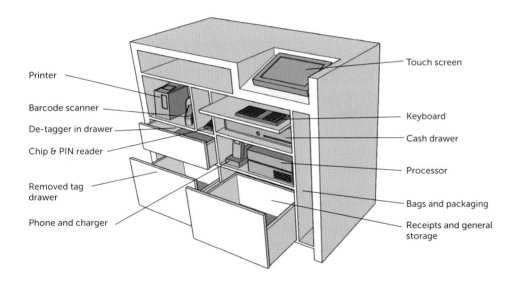

Printer

Barcode scanner

De-tagger in drawer

Chip & PIN reader

Removed tag drawer

Phone and charger

Touch screen

Keyboard

Cash drawer

Processor

Bags and packaging

Receipts and general storage

Typical arrangement of point of sale till equipment.

Multi-bay point of sale with four tills at Abercrombie & Fitch, Eston Town Center, Ohio.

A Cashless Future?

When the coronavirus pandemic hit Europe in the spring of 2020, those retailers who were permitted to keep trading began to decline cash payments. The desire to protect staff from exposure to the virus probably did more to hasten the demise of cash than the launch of any app-based payment system. Stores that trade cashlessly need to be able to process digital payments across a variety of platforms, not only card payments but also Apple Pay and Android Pay. The POS hardware should, at least for the time being, include contactless, chip and pin and magnetic strip readers. As it becomes common practice to email receipts, the printer will no doubt go the way of the cash drawer, with perhaps a back-up facility located in the back of house area. The cashless approach therefore has the potential not only to declutter the POS desk but also to change the retailer's relationship with the customer when a sale is transacted. Rather than the customer bringing their purchases to the POS, the transaction can be carried out anywhere in the store.

People-Counting and Monitoring

When retail anthropologist Paco Underhill began his work in the 1980s to investigate and interpret customer behaviour in stores, his research was conducted through observation on the shop floor. The research methods of Underhill's company Envirosell developed with the advent of home video recording technology but it remained observational research with vast amounts of data to be collated and interpreted by his team. Simple automated people-counters, relying on an infrared beam which was broken when somebody walked across its path, were introduced in the early 2000s and delivered quite accurate counts of the number of people entering and exiting the store. Whilst Envirosell's work aimed to explain to retailers how and why customers shopped as they did, the people-counter's purpose was simply to track numbers so that footfall could be monitored; from that data, the retailer's conversion rate was extrapolated.

As we will see, the technology available to retailers to monitor and interpret customer movement and

Stylish cashless and cardless vending at The Drug Store, New York.

behaviour has developed rapidly over recent years. Nevertheless, people-counters with limited functions remain useful to retailers who wish to collect basic footfall data.

Thermal People-Counters

This type of device uses body heat to track the presence of customers and their direction of movement. Thermal people-counters can return high degrees of accuracy as they are not adversely affected by bright sunlight, darkness or highly reflective backgrounds. They can be mounted over the store entrance and at a range of heights and with various fields of view. The devices return results over Bluetooth and because the data is anonymous, there are few or no issues arising over data protection or privacy.

Stereo Video

This device can be discreet when mounted above the store's entrance doors. It comprises two cameras which simultaneously record data as customers pass below. An algorithm uses data from the two points of view; it compares the two edited images, searches for matching details and, based on the result, calculates and creates a three-dimensional model, determining the presence and position of the customer's head. This allows the counter to filter out unwanted objects such as children in buggies, shopping bags or false data such as shadows. The data can be returned over Bluetooth and is of a high level of accuracy. As well as showing the number of people passing through the door, kinetic heat maps can be created to show customer routes. As with thermal devices, the data returned is anonymous. A similar device, mono video, compares changes in images to track movement. It offers similar functionality to stereo video, although with far less accuracy.

The means of tracking customer movement has developed considerably beyond the task of recording footfall and new technologies now allow retailers to collect far greater amounts of data on their customers.

Wi-Fi

The almost universal possession of smartphones by customers can be exploited to track their movement in the store. Before being acquired by WeWork in early 2019, Euclid Analytics developed a system that measured the signals between the shopper's smartphone and the store's wi-fi antenna that allowed them to map the location of the smartphone, and hence its owner, within the store. Even when not connected to the store's wi-fi, the system can gather unique identification codes sent out by smartphones when they search for networks. This enables stores to identify repeat customers and to learn the time that elapses between repeat visits. Because the smartphone's owner is unaware that their phone is being tracked, there are naturally concerns over privacy and the use to which the data is put. Where customers volunteer personal information to access the store's free wi-fi the data available to the store is much wider, as is the opportunity for the customer to control how the data is used, at least in theory. Stores with this level of insight into customer behaviour and their spending history have the ability to target offers and promotions, both within the store and online.

Analytics

Retailers are increasingly turning to analytics to monitor and understand customer behaviour. This approach can be taken without the need to install new hardware, but rather by using the data already gathered by the store's CCTV system.

CASE STUDY: AURA VISION

Aura Vision's founders did not come into the industry from a retail background but rather through their PhD research under Professor Mark Nixon at the University of Southampton. Professor Nixon's work on gait recognition, which can be used to identify somebody's demographic group through an analysis of how they walk, was developed to recognize other traits such as hair and clothing styles. The software references a large but anonymous data set and uses deep learning to continually improve accuracy as more data is added. Having initially trialled the application in the Students' Union at the university, the first retail application was in London in a large multi-brand footwear retailer.

Within the store, data is captured by the store's existing CCTV cameras and Aura Vision's ethos is to be hardware-agnostic so that their analytics do not require or rely on hardware from a specific man-ufacturer. Ideally, the camera should be a static IP camera, set up to support in-store security with the field of vision and resolution installed for that purpose. The software analyses a sequence of images picked up by the camera and processes it, just as humans decode what they see in the real world using observation, memory and assumption. The artificial intelligence applied can thus determine demographic information from partial data; for example when the object is obscured, a person's face is not visible or the image blurred. The system's accuracy is 95 per cent when determining gender and 85–90 per cent for age. The results on adult age demographics fall into seven groups, each one spanning ten years.

Whilst it is useful for retailers to receive data on their customer demographics, the system's true value is when it is used to support in-depth store analytics. The work pioneered by Paco Underhill on customer behaviour is still important to retailers, particularly because of the depth of insight revealed through observation and interview, but analytics driven by artificial intelligence offers retailers an insight into customer behaviour simultaneously across many stores and throughout the trading day. This allows a comparison of similar stores in order to understand why they might trade differently and to a different customer demographic. Within the store, retailers have an insight into customer journeys through the store and can quickly adjust and test product layouts and even the positioning of sales assistants. This has been determined by Aura Vision as having an effect on conversion rates. Retailers plan and operate their stores relying on a good amount of received wisdom, such as the customer's inclination to make a left turn or to require a few steps beyond the threshold to adjust their senses to the store's environment before they begin to seek out merchandise. Analytics allow these retail theories to be tested, not just in general but in respect of targeted demographic groups. Is there a danger that the use of analytics will ultimately make all stores feel the same, with the same store-planning philosophy underpinning every decision? Not necessarily so, because the use of analytics now allows retailers to understand far more about their customer base. Stores, therefore, have no excuse to follow the path of 'one size fits all' and can be designed to appeal to demographic groups that might have been overlooked or unappreciated using traditional metrics of people counting and observation. Analytics can be valuable in supporting experiential store visits, promoting interactive products and offering a more personalized experience. Using analytics to understand how long a customer may have to wait to be served or to make a payment should only lead to enhancing the level of service.

Overcrowding

Overcrowding

Overcrowding

A) 3 Overcrowding hotspots detected ⚠

Proximity tracking using anonymized data by Aura Vision. (Photo: Aura Vision)

Naturally, customers could be concerned that, as they enter the store under the watchful gaze of the CCTV system, their gait, clothes and physical features are being analysed and the data fed back to the retailer. In these circumstances, should we have concerns over risks to our privacy? Aura Vision's CEO, Dr Daniel Martinho-Corbishley, explains that the system relies entirely on an anonymized data set with no link to individual sales transactions. The analytics have no requirement to identify an individual, nor is this possible through the system's configuration. The data is analysed in the store with no requirement to export it to a remote location for processing. Because no individual is identifiable, no personal data can be gathered, misused or misappropriated. Dr Martinho-Corbishley said, 'Aura Vision was launched in 2017, when Europe was gearing up to introduce General Data Protection Regulation (GDPR). We made the decision early on when we designed the system, that it was not to identify anyone and that all data is aggregated' (personal interview with the author, 15 May 2020, unpublished).

The future for analytics and the deep learning that lies behind these systems is interesting. The social distancing requirements that came about as a result of the Covid-19 pandemic forced retailers to think again about capacity, internal circulation routes and occupancy densities. Analytics can support this work with immediate data showing circulation heat maps and how well distancing measures are being applied. For retailers wishing to adapt quickly, analytics will prove a very valuable tool in their decision making.

The design and construction of a retail
store requires close collaboration and
good teamwork. (Photo: Hyphen)

Chapter Nine

Delivering the Project

SO FAR WE HAVE CONSIDERED THE DESIGN OF the store, its component parts and the materials used in its realization. In this chapter we will look at the process of delivering a store, from the initial concept through to the store's opening. The store designer may choose to take responsibility for the project throughout, or more likely will delegate certain phases of work to other professionals. As well as creative design input, expertise is needed in project management, cost control and the management of construction contracts. A successful project therefore requires the collaboration between a large team, with each member having their specific role to play. Like any design and construction project it is important that the client sets a clear brief for the team and that timescales and budgets are understood. This chapter sets out the key organizational principles for the delivery of a retail project and whilst the timescales will vary according to the location, size and complexity of the project, the principles will nevertheless apply.

THE PROJECT TEAM

The consultant team working in store design contains a mix of disciplines which are not usually encountered in other sectors, particularly the roles of executive architect and local architect. In a traditional architectural project, for example the design and construction of an office building or a residential building, the architect will contribute to the feasibility study, develop the concept design, prepare the tender and construction documents and act as the contract administrator (CA). Retail design differs in how these roles are split up, but equally the team roles described below can be considered fluid and it is not uncommon for individuals to occupy more than one role, for example with project management and cost management duties also falling to the executive architect.

Concept Designer

Retailers investing in brick and mortar stores are not just looking for selling space but also seeking to give physical expression to their brand. When a major fashion house appoints a new creative director and the brand is led in a new direction, it is not just the character of the collections that changes but everything that supports the brand's retail business. The job of developing the design of the store to reflect a brand's personality and vision belongs to the concept designer. Their ideas may be conceived around an imaginary space, exploring design ideas, materials and space-making in the abstract. As the design develops, and usually in close contact with the brand's own creative team, mock-ups, models and images test the concept until it is sufficiently developed as a new store design. At this stage, a site might be selected to trial-run the design. The concept designer's value to the brand is being able to imagine new spaces and give them a physical form. It is rare, though, for the creative team and the concept designer to wish to invest further time in realizing all parts of the design in full detail or in overseeing the project through to completion. More usually, the development of the design is handed on to the executive architect.

Store Development Manager

Where brands are engaged in the development of many sites, they often manage this process internally through their own store development department. The store development manager oversees the process from concept to store opening, making the key external team appointments and acting as the voice of the client. Often the store development team will play a role in the delivery of projects, possibly supporting the construction phase in a project management role and placing orders with specialist contractors and suppliers appointed by the brand but not included in the main construction contract.

Executive Architect

The executive architect, or architect of record as this role is known in North America, has the job of developing the concept design to a level of detail that allows the project to be constructed. Their work will often begin with the site survey and site investigation. The site investigation might verify planning restrictions or other local issues that could directly affect the fit of the design concept to the site. The executive architect brings their knowledge of planning, building regulations and other statutory consents to support the concept designer who can then adjust the design to suit the site constraints. Once the concept design for the site is frozen, the executive architect can begin to develop more detailed designs.

Typically, the executive architect will begin their work by re-drawing the scheme themselves, using the dimensional survey information for their base drawings. From this point onwards, the executive architect's role typically follows the duties set out in the RIBA's Plan of Work or the local equivalent if outside the UK. The executive architect will develop the details necessary to complete the design, perhaps making periodic checks with the concept designer to ensure that their interpretation is correct. As the

design develops, the executive architect might take responsibility for areas of the design not addressed by the concept design, such as the back of house areas, the storefront and services coordination. The role demands the ability to see where gaps lie in design information and to step in and supplement it where it is missing. The executive architect will take responsibility for the project through to completion although their cost management and contract administration duties may be split with a project manager.

Local Architect

Many brands who have developed a successful concept will wish to open or refurbish stores in several locations and often over a short period of time. The design team may well be asked to complete projects in countries where they have little or no experience in the local market. This requires knowledge of local statutory regulations and contracting methods. In many countries, construction permit submissions can only be made by licensed professions, usually architects or interior architects and so the involvement of a local architect is needed to support the project. Usually the local architect's first duty is to sense-check the concept design for local building code compliance. They will then support the design team in their work, perhaps liaising with statutory authorities, local landlords and potential contractors. Where drawings and documents are required in the local language, they undertake or commission the required translations too. Throughout this process, the executive architect retains overall project responsibility and the local architect's role might cease once the country-specific matters have been dealt with.

Project Manager

Whilst this role can sometimes be undertaken by the brand itself, it may equally be taken up by an external consultant who undertakes the job on a project-by-project basis. The project manager is responsible for controlling the programme (time schedule) and the budget, and may also be responsible for coordinating direct orders placed by the brand in support of the project. The project manager often acts as the contract administrator if this duty is not undertaken by the architect.

Cost Manager

Where the project is large or complicated, responsibility for establishing the budget and managing the project spend may be allocated to a specialist. In the UK, the quantity surveyor (QS) undertakes this role, but elsewhere this position can be filled by another member of the team such as the executive architect or the project manager.

Services Engineer

The services engineer, also referred to as the M&E (mechanical and electrical) engineer, plays a vital role in ensuring that the store is adequately heated and cooled and that the electrical systems adequately meet the store's needs. As ducts, conduits and cable trays must be threaded through the store, close coordination is required across the design team to ensure that the services are integrated into the design. The services engineering role is usually split into different disciplines.

Mechanical Engineering

This role concerns the design of the heating, cooling and ventilation systems with the goal of ensuring that a comfortable environment is maintained within the store. This is achieved through controlling the heating and cooling of the space as well as regulating the circulation of fresh air.

Electrical Engineering

As well as power and lighting circuit design, the electrical engineer's scope may include data, security and building automation. Whilst the design and installation of specialist equipment may lie with others, the design of the wiring infrastructure and its coordination usually rests with the electrical engineer.

Public Health Engineering

Plumbing and drainage works might not be a large part of the store's design, but even the simplest will probably include a staff toilet or kitchen and their design is the responsibility of the public health engineer.

Lighting Designer

No well-designed store can disregard good lighting and the responsibility for achieving it rests with the lighting designer, whose brief will include the store's ambient lighting as well as display and fixture lighting that supports the concept designer's vision. Having developed a design that supports the aims of the concept designer, the lighting designer is then responsible for the specification of the fittings and will support the store's visual merchandising team in the positioning and focussing of luminaires prior to the store opening.

Structural Engineer

The structural engineer is more likely to play a role in larger projects, particularly where these involve substantial alterations to existing buildings. As well as ensuring that structural alterations are designed to maintain the structural integrity of the building, the structural engineer often has a key role to play in the design of major interventions forming part of the retail design, such as a new staircase or a storefront, particularly where the design concept calls for unusual structural solutions or construction methods.

Fire Engineer

It may not always be possible to comply with the guidance of approved documents to achieve building regulations approval, particularly where the store's design or the building in which the store is located is complicated or unusual. In these cases, a solution to provide means of escape, smoke evacuation and fire protection is designed by a fire engineer from first principles.

Other Roles Within the Brand's Organization

Whilst the brand's interests may be represented by the store development manager during the design and construction phases, he or she will usually seek information and guidance from other members of the brand's organization.

Store Manager

This is the person ultimately responsible for the running of the finished store. Their duties include ordering and replenishing stock, managing staff and taking responsibility for the store's day-to-day trading activity. Whilst not usually involved in the early store design phases, their contribution to setting up the store and organizing stock prior to trade can be invaluable.

Security Manager

The design team will usually take their brief for physical security and loss prevention measures from the brand's security manager. The security manager will advise on matters such as the security rating for the storefront, stock loss prevention, CCTV camera positions and their specifications.

Visual Merchandiser

The visual merchandising team plays a critical role in merchandising the store prior to opening. As well as the display of product, its members are responsible for the design and set-up of display pieces such as mannequin groups, window displays and promotions. Whereas the store design team's role generally ends shortly after the store's opening, the visual merchandiser will visit the store periodically thereafter to update product collections and displays.

The Construction Team

In most cases the design of a new store proceeds through the work of the design team until the project is tendered or bid to potential contractors. Once appointed, the contractor or contractors join the team and take responsibility for construction of the store.

Main Contractor

The contractor, often a specialist shopfitter, is given the job to build the store in accordance with the drawings and specifications prepared by the design team and usually for a fixed price. Because the range of construction skills required on retail is wide the contractor will often appoint subcontractors to work on the project on their behalf, particularly for the installation of services or for unusual finishes. On larger projects it is not uncommon for the main contractor to subcontract the majority of the building work to specialist firms and to add value to the project through their management and coordination skills.

Millwork Contractor

The manufacture and installation of retail display fixtures has evolved into a specialism beyond the scope of most main contractors. Brands have discovered that by separating the production of display furniture and awarding supply contracts to specialist millwork manufacturers they can ensure a more consistent quality and a keener price. This is particularly the case where a brand is considering the supply of multiple stores. The store's millwork is fabricated off-site in the millworker's production facility and delivered once the main contractor has prepared the site for installation. In most cases, the millwork manufacturer's own team is responsible for assembly and installation.

Specialist Subcontractors and Suppliers

Works to complete the store do not end with the general contractor and the millworker. There may be specialist finishes to apply or artworks that are commissioned by the brand. The timely installation of these and other client direct orders requires careful coordination amongst the project delivery team.

PROJECT DELIVERY

Project teams divide their work over the course of a project into distinct work stages. By having defined stages with a beginning and an end, teams can work to an agreed programme with each member aware of the work they must complete before progressing to the next stage. The most widely used system of work stages in the UK is the one published by the Royal Institute of British Architects (RIBA). The RIBA Plan of Work was first launched in 1963 and is a useful tool because it looks beyond simply defining work stages for the purpose of the architect's fees and scope, but rather attempts to map out the principal tasks at each work stage. It sets out who in the design team is involved and the information to be released or exchanged at the end of each stage. The RIBA Plan of Work also attempts to overlay strategies for sustainability and procurement. We will now look at the process of store design and construction through the prism of the RIBA Plan of Work 2020.

When the Plan of Work was relaunched in 2020, the RIBA noted that 'In many countries there is no formal set process for designing a building. "The way to do it" is unwritten and unrecorded.' Globally that might be the case, but actually most European countries have their own systems of long standing; for instance the scope of six work stages defined by the Architects' Council of Europe, or the German *Honorarordnung für Architekten und Ingenieure* (HOAI) which defines in detail the basis of architectural and engineering fees during eight work stages. Store designers working frequently with North American clients will no doubt be familiar with the American Institute of Architects (AIA) Five Phases of Architecture that are commonly referred to throughout the industry in the US: Schematic Design (SD), Design Development (DD), Contract Documents (CD), Bidding and Contract Administration (CA). It is beyond the scope of this book to explore the merits of each system, although the principles of beginning the project with pre-design activities and finishing with occupation and aftercare are common to all.

Stage 0: Strategic Definition

This stage lies at the beginning of the design process and involves the retailer developing the project's business case. This could be prompted by the end of a lease period, opportunities to expand the brand into new markets, or the recognition that their existing store is no longer offering what it is needed in size or layout. As the business case is being developed, the brand representatives may review previous projects, visit potential store locations and develop an outline budget. Larger brands looking to new locations may commission their own market surveys or study the demographics of potential locations.

Site Location

All well-managed brands know that the location of the store can be as important to the success of a store as the merchandise on offer or the interior design of the store. A brand may be embarking on a significant expansion in a new country or region and will commit resources to investigating those markets, the proximity of competitors and the availability of prime sites. There may also be the need to consider warehouse facilities, distribution and fulfilment, all of which can take a considerable time for a brand to assess. Having identified the target locations, the brands will work closely with specialist retail agents and major landlords to locate specific sites that will be available during the brand's development cycle.

Lease Negotiation

It is unusual for brands to own the buildings from which they trade although there are, of course, exceptions. Assuming that a brand is leasing a mall unit or a high street property, there will be a period of negotiation to finalize the lease, principally to agree the lease area, the rental price and any subsequent variations. It is important for the brand as lessor to understand the landlord's obligations, such as preparatory works prior to taking possession of the site, and also its obligation on departure. The requirement to remove shop fit-out on termination of the lease is often overlooked by exiting tenants.

Calculating Area in Terms of Zone A (ITZA)

When assessing the value of a lease on a high street retail property in the UK, the ITZA method is often applied. This method originated in the 1950s as a way to account for the greater value of retail space lying adjacent to the storefront, the reason being that this is the area of the store most likely to appeal to the passing customer. Whilst other calculations can be used in lease negotiation, the traditional method is to calculate the rental by zones of diminishing value starting with the first, zone A, which extends from the storefront into the store to a depth of 20 feet (6.1m). The next, zone B, extends a further 20 feet and the process is repeated as far as zone D if the store has a very deep plan. The value of each zone is reckoned to be half that of its predecessor and so if zone A is valued at £42/m², zone B will be calculated at £21/m² and zone C at £10.50 and so on. The simple ITZA-based valuation is applicable to ground-floor retail space and assumes a storefront to one side only. Basement or upper floors are usually valued at a lower rent and usually as a small fraction of the zone A value. An experienced property surveyor will also take into account particular local conditions such as L-shaped plans or corner sites where the storefront wraps around two sides of the store.

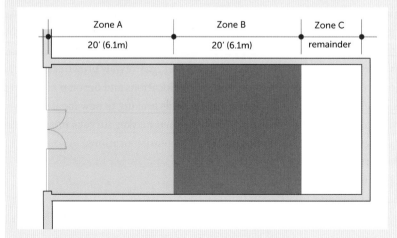

Zone A	Zone B	Zone C
20' (6.1m)	20' (6.1m)	remainder

Calculating area in terms of zone A (ITZA).

Stage 1: Preparation and Briefing

Having established its requirements and developed a business case, the brand should have now established if a project is viable and will be ready to appoint the design team. In most cases, the design team comprises independent consultants although larger brands often employ their own in-house store designers and project managers who work alongside external consultants employed on a project-by-project basis. The benefit of this relationship is that the brand's own team members have a detailed knowledge of the brand concept, product range, fixtures, finishes and suppliers, whereas the external consultants bring specific expert knowledge of construction, permitting, engineering and so on.

The project brief should set out the store's spatial requirements and these may need to be tested through feasibility studies looking at the physical condition of the selected site, the site area, floor-to-ceiling heights and other constraints. At this stage site surveys are undertaken to collect as much data as possible. Despite the fact that retail sites change hands often and are therefore refurbished frequently (typically a store fit-out has a life of four to seven years), reliable information about the site is often hard to obtain. In the UK, where town planning applications and approvals are available in the public domain, this can often be a good starting point in tracing drawings of the current or past works. If as-built record drawings are available from the landlord or current tenant these are useful but should not be relied on without a prior check on site. A site survey has two main aims, the first being a visual inspection of the premises noting any significant matters that are likely to impact on the project. This will include a check of the building fabric, including the condition of any elements that are to be retained. It is wise at this stage to have the MEP engineer undertake a survey of the condition of the existing building services, including existing drain runs, external plant areas, incoming electrical supplies and any other services that would prove difficult and costly not to retain.

The second part of the survey is a dimensional survey which measures and records the physical space to produce drawings that accurately depict the current size and shape of the site. For small and uncomplicated sites this can easily be accomplished using a measuring tape and a laser measure, but for complicated sites, or sites where the existing shopfit makes it difficult to access ceiling or wall voids, a point cloud survey may be worthwhile commissioning. Rather than producing a two-dimensional drawing as a traditional measurement survey does, the point cloud survey produces a 3D model from a record of thousands of datapoints taken using a 3D laser scan to capture the surface of the surveyed space. The survey will also pick up furniture, fixtures and any merchandise present. This might mean that the designer has to undertake a fair degree of editing to achieve a useful result but the final output is an accurate 3D model of the space from which plan and section drawings can be derived.

Within the world of retail, shopfits change frequently and it is often the case that dimensional site surveys are taken when the store is still trading and certainly before the existing shopfit has been removed. It is therefore wise to remeasure the site as soon as it has been stripped out. This allows for the verification of any assumptions made during the first visits or the opportunity to adjust the design to suit the actual site condition.

As the design team is appointed the project manager should develop a responsibility matrix so that every member of the team is aware of their role in the project. This is particularly important when a brand's team is working alongside external consultants and the traditional client–consultant relationship lines are blurred.

Brand Design Guidelines

Where a brand embarks on a major roll-out of projects or refurbishments, it is important that the standard of the design is maintained and that details, finishes and materials are consistent. To this end, the final concept may well be captured in a brand guideline pack which is issued to the design team as the benchmark against which to work. The pack usually comprises drawings explaining the principles of the store's spatial planning as well as the key details. The design guide should include typical examples of all display furniture in sufficient detail to allow the design to be developed in accordance with the concept. In addition to drawings, the pack may also include a sample box allowing locally sourced materials to be checked against a control set. A schedule of employer's requirements can be useful in defining the brand's expectations for the performance of the proposed building services.

Stage 2: Concept Design

As we have seen, the concept designer may be working inside the brand or may be selected as an outside consultant appointed to introduce a new look and feel to the brand's stores. The concept designer's brief is to understand the ethos of the brand, its values and its offer, products or merchandise. The store design, if it is successful, expresses the brand and creates an environment where the brand's products are displayed to best effect.

Scale models are used to test the design and communicate the concept. (Photo: Hyphen)

The concept design is true to the brief whilst acknowledging and recognizing the constraints and physical limits that have been identified through the surveys. Where the concept design is based on a set of brand design guidelines, the concept will identify how these can be made to work for the actual site and where and if they must flex. The concept design should include inputs from the design team's MEP engineer, the structural engineer and any specialists with relevant insight into other design influences, such as a historic buildings specialist or a fire engineer.

The concept design is typically developed through plans and sketches but as it begins to crystallize, models (both traditional and virtual) are used to present the design and a sample board may be used to demonstrate and explain the proposed materials. Based on the concept design, the cost plan and project programme can be updated and used to test the assumptions of the budget and the brief. An outline specification may now be issued to define the standards envisaged for the main construction elements such as the principal finishes and materials. The concept design stage should then be signed off by the client before proceeding to the next work stage. This avoids future misunderstanding, uncertainty and abortive work.

Whist the RIBA Plan of Work envisages that the submissions of applications for town planning fall within Stage 3, time constraints (and particularly the length of time the local planning authority (LPA) requires to determine an application) force this to be addressed earlier in the project. Where the LPA's interest is limited to façade works or signage alone, there is merit in fast-tracking these aspects of the design to gain time during the approval process.

Stage 3: Spatial Coordination

In this work stage, the concept is developed into a spatially accurate design in compliance with the building regulations and other statutory codes or guidance. The key deliverable from this work stage is a coordinated design which includes proposed building services, structural interventions and the architecture of the design. In working towards the completion of this stage, the design team tests and validates the concept design, identifying spatial conflicts and clashes between the work of the design team's disciplines.

Whilst it is very much the norm that the new store design will be constructed within an existing building, this in no way negates the need to apply and obtain statutory approvals. In the UK, these include consents for town planning and building control and most façade signage will also require a consent to display advertising. In city locations, particularly in the main shopping streets of Europe, historic or listed building consents will also be required. The statutory approval process varies between countries and it is important for the brand to understand the process, how long it will take to achieve approvals and what, if any, works can be undertaken prior to approval being granted.

Stage 3 should be completed with checks of the budget, possibly preparing an initial elemental analysis of the design to produce a more detailed cost plan. Where suppliers of long-lead materials or components have been identified, quotes should be sought and it may be necessary to place orders in advance of the main tender process to ensure that the required delivery dates can be achieved.

Stage 4: Technical Design

The objective in preparing technical design information is to produce a comprehensive document set from which the store can be constructed. This includes works such as display furniture, which is typically manufactured off site. Responsibility for completing the technical design might reside across several parties such as specialist contractors as well as the original design team. This is particularly true where the store design contains specialist installations such as lifts or sprinkler systems which the design team is not usually equipped to address. Where the design requires subcontract design, the responsibility matrix should be updated and the extent and boundaries of design liability agreed and recorded.

The bid, or set of tender documents, is used to seek priced offers from suitably qualified contractors. The document set comprises drawings, specifications and other relevant pieces of information that the bidding contractor will need in order to understand the project such as the programme, the status of statutory consents, any site constraints and information

A photo-realistic image of a retail interior can be used to verify the final design before the project is bid to contractors. (Photo: Hyphen)

on health and safety. The bidders' prices are ideally returned on a pricing schedule, allowing for easy checking and comparison between offers. Depending on the custom and practice of the country in which the job is bid, the bidders may measure the work themselves, meaning that they estimate the extent of any work item as they price it. In some cases, one of the design team will prepare an estimate of quantities so that all bidders make their offers against a common schedule of quantities. This responsibility usually falls to the executive architect or the cost manager. In the UK this task sits with a cost specialist called a quantity surveyor.

When bidding a project, there are some good practice principles that should be adopted by teams wishing to obtain the best prices and the most credible bids. Firstly, it is valuable to engage in a pre-qualification exercise to select suitable bidders prior to the issue of tenders. The purpose of this is to establish if the bidders have the requisite knowledge, resource and interest to take on the project. There is little point in having a contractor bid a project if they have no capacity to start the job. Having established the long list of suitable bidders, the most suitable should be invited to bid. It is important to gauge the right number of bidders: too few and there is a risk that there is no chance for a competitive bid to emerge; too many and the bidders feel that they have only a limited opportunity to win the work and this blunts their willingness to be competitive. For a typical retail project, if there is such a thing, a bid pool of three to five is usually the right number. Finally, and when there are project time constraints, it is tempting to press bidders to return their offers within days. However straightforward the pricing has been made, through clear documents and by providing measured schedules, the bidders need time to price. It is almost certain that a contractor's bid will include subcontracted works and time is required for these to be sifted out, bid to the relevant firms, negotiated and then incorporated back into the main bid. The deadline for receiving bids should be clearly stated and adhered to. The returned bids should be assessed for accuracy and compared with one another. If the standard of all submissions is the same, then the lowest price bid is typically the winner, although if a bidder is able to offer something that sets them apart, such as an improvement on the programme, they may be preferred for the job. The bid process does not guarantee that the lowest price is awarded the contract. The aim is to appoint the bidder with the best overall bid. Once the winning bidder has been identified, they enter into a contract with the client, referred to in the contract as the employer.

The works stages discussed thus far have assumed traditional methods of procurement. The design team produces tender documents against which potential contractors bid competitively at Stage 4. Other methods of procurement exist, but the relatively small size of retail contracts makes alternative methods less common.

Management Contracting

In this method, the management contractor is appointed much earlier in the design process, usually on completion of Stage 2. The client appoints all the subcontractors and specialist contractors required to build the project, but hands responsibility for the management and coordination of subcontractors over to the management contractor. Because the management contractor is appointed early in the design process, their experience can be brought to bear on the project, improving the cost and the buildability of proposals whilst still in the design stage. This method is probably most appropriate on large, complicated projects where the brand wishes to gain as much time as possible. This method requires a knowledgeable and well-resourced client because they retain the contractual relationships with the individual subcontractors.

Design and Build Contracting

Where the brand wishes to place responsibility for the delivery of their project with a single party, this method of procurement can be used. The contractor is appointed early, possibly from the outset of the project. Because the project at this stage does not have sufficient detail to cost, the design and build contractor may be selected through the competitive bidding of preliminaries or simply by negotiation. Preliminaries are those items not directly related to the construction of the project itself and include management costs, site set-up costs, overhead and profit. The contractor is responsible for employing the design team themselves or may already have this expertise in-house. Where the client wishes to control the concept design process, the store designer may begin their role employed by the client and then have their employment transferred to the design and build contractor to complete the design, a process known as novation. Where the brand's store design standards are well understood or established, this method of procurement can be an effective way to procure projects. Many brands prefer to procure projects through a single point of contact and on the basis of a lump sum price. However, there is a risk that without the independent oversight of the design team the contractor does not deliver to the quality anticipated by the brand. For this reason, the employer's requirements which set out the project standards must be clear from the outset.

Stage 5: Manufacturing and Construction

Ideally, the bid set is the basis for the contract documents, against which the agreed price is fixed. However, there may have been some design development in the interim; for example, if further information comes to light about site conditions or if the winning bidder has suggestions to improve the project or reduce cost. Once the contractor is appointed they will require a period of mobilization, usually no more than four weeks, during which they prepare to take possession of the site, order materials and plan labour. Where the site has a prominent location, the site hoarding should be given significant consideration

to ensure that the opportunity to advertise the forthcoming store is not lost. The mobilization period can also be used to obtain the required consents for the erection of the hoarding and the display of advertising material that will be applied to the hoarding.

Construction Contracts

In the UK, a number of standard construction contracts are available, the best known being those published by the Joint Contracts Tribunal (JCT). Some clients prefer to have their legal advisors draft a bespoke form of contract but this should be discouraged because it results in a contract which is unfamiliar to the contractor and, in all likelihood, weighted in favour of the employer. The advantage in using the JCT standard forms of contract is that these have been developed by a cross-section of construction industry representatives and are therefore deemed to allocate risk fairly between the contracting parties. The other advantages are speed to agree the contract, reduced costs in preparing contracts and a solid body of industry experience and case law against which to decide disputes. The contract administrator (CA) is named in the contract and their main duties include monitoring progress on site, considering claims and agreeing variations, certifying the value of work at various stages and determining at what point the works have been completed. The CA role is usually taken by the project architect or project manager but, whoever is appointed, they must administer the contract impartially neither favouring the employer or the contractor in their decision making.

Regular site meetings are held to ensure that the works on site progress smoothly. Depending on the size of the project the contractor may be required to prepare a site progress report in advance of the meeting. This should record actual site progress against the construction programme as well as the status of the procurement of specialist subcontractors and materials. The contractor may also table requests for information (RFIs), valuations and reports on health and safety on site. There is no fixed rule on the

Attractive screening of the construction site presents a smart face to customers. Story at Macy's New York.

contractor is made aware of the extent and times of client-appointed works so that they can schedule them within their own programme. Equally important is that client-appointed trades arriving on site understand that the responsibility for managing health and safety on site remains with the main contractor and so they must follow site rules such as submitting risk and method statements (RAMs) and receiving safety inductions prior to commencing work. An experienced retail contractor understands that a good final result is achieved through positive working relationships between themselves, the sub-contractors and the client-appointed suppliers.

Programming

The importance of opening a project on time is paramount, but no more so than in the retail world. Retailers are often trading to a particularly rigorous calendar with merchandise ordered to suit a specific sales period or season. For this reason, a delay in the opening can be very disruptive to a brand's merchandising and its sales plans. Retail projects therefore require that the construction programme be very closely managed in order to avoid or mitigate delays. Typically, a retail project requires the installation of many elements that are prefabricated or manufactured off site. The construction programme must therefore not only track the activities on site but consider the wider procurement paths for millwork, specialist fittings and materials. Where samples or mock-ups are required in advance of an order being placed, or materials are identified that have long order periods, these time constraints need to be accommodated in the project programme.

Snagging

As the project nears completion, the design team should be offered the opportunity to inspect the works and prepare snag lists. Snag lists, or 'punch lists' as they are known in North America, are quality checks that are made prior to handover. This is the design team's opportunity to check the works for any

frequency of site meetings, nor who should attend, so common sense should prevail. Generally, the more compact the construction programme, the more frequent the need to meet because issues arising on site will require immediate responses.

Client Direct Procurement

Because the eventual character and appearance of the store will closely reflect the retailer's brand, retail clients are more closely involved in the procurement and installation of the store than clients in other sectors. For example, a fashion brand may use a unique stone tile for the flooring of all their stores and are likely to have secured this material from one stone merchant for world-wide distribution. The brand is also likely to have established framework contracts for the procurement of millwork supplied to established designs set out in their store design guide. Other areas where brands are likely to be actively involved in sourcing and procurement are brand signage, loose furniture, luminaires, visual merchandising and artwork. Whilst the brand's direct involvement in such a wide range of items ensures that they control procurement costs and quality, this degree of involvement means that the risk in delivering large areas of the project scope shifts from contractor to employer. The JCT Standard Building Contract makes provision for this activity but it is imperative that the defects and have the contractor rectify them before the works are accepted as practically complete. The services installation should be commissioned at this stage, with life safety systems such as fire detection and alarms certified as compliant. The milestone of practical completion triggers various actions in the Standard Building Contract, with the employer now becoming responsible for the insurance and management of the site.

Stage 6: Handover

Practical completion marks the end of the contractor's contractual role on site, but there are further works to be done before the store can open its doors and trade. Time in the programme must be allowed for this important period and the design team should resist the temptation to allocate more time to the contractor for their works if this reduces the time designated for pre-opening activities. The store is likely to require frequent cleaning at this stage as construction dust settles. The contractor's site cleaning prior to handover is unlikely to be adequate come the opening period and specialist cleaning companies with experience of working in retail stores are usually worthwhile engaging at this stage. The brand can now bring stock onto site and begin merchandising the displays. Once the front of house is merchandised and displays and visual merchandising set up, the lighting can be focussed. In parallel, the brand's IT engineers will set up back of house computers, tills, printers and other operational equipment. The design team should ensure that all of the operation and maintenance manuals as well as any relevant instruction manuals are correctly filed and issued to the store manager or the brand's facilities manager. These manuals, which generally exist only in electronic format, should comprise searchable files and include as-built drawings. When plans are made to alter the store in the future, comprehensive information on file will be invaluable to the future design team.

If the brand is involved in a roll-out of further stores the design team should be invited to a 'lessons

The site nears completion: last-minute finishing before handover.

learned' project review aimed at identifying improvements to the quality, speed and cost of future projects.

Stage 7: Use

Under the Standard Building Contract there is a rectification period of six to twelve months after practical completion, during which the contractor repairs shrinkage cracks or faults that occur in the works. At the end of this period, the design team will revisit the store to verify that the remedial works have been completed satisfactorily. Brands with larger stores or with many stores in their portfolio might benefit from a post-occupancy evaluation, the outcomes of which can be used to support future design improvements.

Lush are proud to promote their stance on animal testing. Lush Liverpool. (Photo: Lush)

Chapter Ten

Retail's Future

AS WE ENTERED THE EARLY YEARS OF THE 2020s we saw famous name stores cease trading, leaving empty retail units in their wake and retailers bemoaning online competition. This is not the full story, although it is undoubtedly true that online sales have massively impacted on customers' habits. The coronavirus pandemic had a disruptive effect on the market due to imposed confinement and social distancing which led to a surge in online shopping, particularly amongst those who were more vulnerable to the virus and who might not have previously considered themselves tech-savvy. The requirement to maintain a physical distance and the drastic limits on numbers permitted to enter stores made a mockery of previous design assumptions on capacity. At the time of writing, it is not clear how long it will take for the effects of social distancing to dissipate. Even when the worst of the virus passes, it is possible that social distancing becomes the norm, with a strong cultural resistance to return to the close proximity with fellow customers that was once taken for granted.

The coronavirus pandemic forced retailers to adapt quickly to social distancing and to lower capacities in their stores.

SOCIALLY DISTANCED RETAIL

The experience of confinement, travel restrictions and social distancing are likely to have changed customers' behaviour, if not irrevocably then certainly for the foreseeable future. Consumers have discovered the fragility of supply chains, their own inability to outrun panic buying and the perception that shopping online from home is safer than venturing to the mall or high street. Many retailers found themselves unable to trade from their brick and mortar stores in the spring of 2020 when the UK went into lockdown. For some, this was the final blow that put them out of business, but for others it forced them to switch sales through new and better online stores. There will certainly be some retailers who found that 2020 was the year that their online business became as important (or more so) as the very best store in their estate.

As retail reopened following lockdown, it emerged into a very different world. It was one where customers and sales assistants interacted through a perspex screen, cash was suddenly unwelcome and people accepted the need to queue to gain entry to the store. Some customers were surprised to be asked if they would have their temperature taken but complied out of courtesy and the desire to go shopping again.

For the store planners looking to the future, how should socially distanced retail inform their thinking? Spaciousness and the ability to offer the customer an environment where they can circulate freely without feeling they are confined might inform the store's space planning. If the commercial pressure of online competition once challenged retailers to think about smaller, more efficient stores that were cheaper to build and operate, then this could now be reversed. But if the budgets just aren't available to plan large stores with open circulation and with a low product capacity, what is the alternative? One approach might be that the assortment reduces so that customers visiting the store no longer expect to find a retailer's entire range available. Everyday pieces might be available online only, with the store environment reserved for the exceptional, the customizable, the experiential and the highly desirable. This omnichannel approach will include the ability to deliver quickly and accurately as well as giving the physical stores a purpose to attract customers through experiences that cannot be found online.

The Re-Vision My-Scan™ system allows customers to shop and pay without using the traditional supermarket checkout.

Cashless Shopping?

The rapid demise of cash in the UK and elsewhere was accelerated by the coronavirus. For a period when consumers were confined to their homes, there was an initial spike in ATM use as people sought to hoard cash for an emergency, but as the lockdown continued, the opportunities to spend cash diminished. To prevent the risk of viral infection, many retailers imposed, or at least encouraged, contactless payment when their stores reopened. Professional services company Accenture reported that the use of cash declined by 40 per cent during 2020 and this is likely to be a trend that will not be reversed. Once shoppers stop carrying cash they are unlikely to readopt the habit. Contributing to the declining use of cash are customers using smart phone apps such as Apple Pay and other digital wallets. As well as no longer having to use cash, customers have encountered increasing opportunities to avoid the traditional sales till altogether. RFID technology allows for frictionless transactions of asset-tagged goods and this, supported by camera monitoring and machine-learning, could see 'just walk out' shopping becoming more commonplace. Amazon Go convenience stores are already established in the US and the first Amazon Fresh grocery store using the same technology opened to the general public in late 2020 in Woodland Hills, California.

In Europe, the company Re-Vision has developed the My-Scan™ system which allows supermarket customers to scan and bag as they go. The system also uses machine learning to direct customers in the store, help with store navigation and tailor offers and discounts to the individual. Underlying all of these technologies is the bargain between retailer and consumer where the customer trades data on their preferences, their shopping patterns, their demographic and their level of wealth for the convenience of queue-free, cashless shopping.

SUSTAINABLE RETAIL DESIGN

The awareness amongst consumers that their choices have profound consequences for the environment is now so firmly rooted that retailers who disregard or appear to disregard this truth can appear out of touch and irrelevant. In the UK, shoppers quickly embraced the small levy on single-use plastic bags that was introduced in October 2015 and there is an ongoing drive across the entire sector to reduce packaging and the waste it produces.

It seems likely that, as awareness grows, consumers will also look to the store environment to see how a brand's attitude to sustainability is reflected. It is therefore unacceptable to embark on design projects which knowingly use methods and materials that cause irrevocable damage to the environment. It should go without saying that the store designer has a duty to ensure that the construction materials specified are sourced responsibly. The Building Research Establishment (BRE) states that responsible sourcing is 'demonstrated through an ethos of supply chain management and product stewardship and encompasses social, economic and environmental dimensions.'

BRE Global's Framework Standard for Responsible Sourcing (BES 6001) is a published standard against which material manufactures can check that the constituent materials have been responsibly resourced. The standard seeks to set standards of governance, supply chain management and environmental and social responsibility. Responsible sourcing is just one aspect of sustainability in construction and many manufacturers have now adapted their manufacturing processes to make them more sustainable. This includes measures to reduce the amount of non-renewable material in products and to reduce the adverse impact on the environment when used. Many products available to the specifier are now lauded for their use of recycled materials or with their future recycling path considered. Examples include worktops made from ground or crushed glass salvaged from recycled glass bottles, and plastic sheets made from recycled low-density polythene (LDPE). Whilst beneficial for the reduction of landfill or incineration, the recycling of waste into construction products is a linear process; that is to say, the resulting product cannot itself be wholly recycled, for example the bonding agents added to recyclables in a sheet material. William McDonough and Michael Braudgart addressed this in their book *Cradle to Cradle: Remaking the Way We Make Things* with the principle that 'everything

is a resource for something else'. They propose that, just as in the natural world, the waste of one system becomes the food for another, so materials can be engineered to follow a similar cycle. Materials are therefore either recyclable or return to the soil as uncontaminated biological nutrients. The goal is to achieve a circular economy and the authors look beyond the production of materials alone to recognize the need for the use of renewable energy in production processes.

THE STORE'S PURPOSE

Stores that are opened in the future will only be of relevance if they succeed in offering something that cannot be gained from the customers' experiences online. The ability to incorporate brick and mortar stores into a brand's omnichannel offer will become ever more important as retailers compete for customers in the coming years. The store cannot be merely a depository of product or website shopping translated into physical form. Retailers and their store-planning teams must find a purpose to their new stores if they are to prosper. We are already seeing how purpose-driven stores can differentiate a brand in the market, whether that purpose is to allow seamless, cash-free and contact-free convenience or to offer experience-led retail that excites and intrigues the customer. The design that supports these new stores is likely to be more flexible and more readily adaptable to change as we recalibrate the retail world in the aftermath of coronavirus. There is a lot for the store designer to consider as they begin to plan our retail future but finding the purpose of the store should be the foundation on which the new store is built.

AHU: air-handling unit.

Back of house: the areas of the store supporting operations, not usually seen by, or encountered by, the customer.

Brick and mortar store: a physical store as opposed to an online or virtual store.

Cash wrap: a variation on the POS, usually where the items sold have a requirement to be wrapped, packaged or bagged as part of the sale.

Ceiling device plan: an RCP showing all lighting, grilles, sprinkler heads, smoke detectors and so on.

Click and collect: the service offered by retailers allowing customers to collect goods from stores that have been ordered in advance online.

dB: decibel.

Demise: (1) (legal) abbreviated from 'demised premises' and referring to the area of the site leased to the retailer or owned by them; (2) the end or failure of something.

Dilapidations: works required under a lease to maintain or reinstate the site when the retailer exits at the end of the lease. This may include the requirement to remove their fit-out and to return the site to grey box or white box condition.

FCU: fan coil unit.

Front of house: the areas of the store where merchandise is displayed and sold and open to the customer.

GFA: gross floor area.

GIA: gross internal area.

Grey box: a raw, undeveloped site with no finishes, although possibly provided with utilities and services connection points.

Haute couture: fashion derived from made-to-measure clothes for private clients and therefore exclusive and expensive.

IP: Internet Protocol.

ITZA: In Terms of Zone A: a method for valuing retail premises.

JCT: Joint Contracts Tribunal.

MDF: medium-density fibreboard: a man-made sheet material formed from wood fibres and synthetic resin, bonded under high heat and pressure; often used in the manufacture of fixtures.

MEP: mechanical, electrical and plumbing engineer.

Millwork: in common usage this refers to any manufactured joinery pieces commissioned for the display of a store's merchandise.

Omnichannel: an approach to retail that integrates an online sales presence with a brand's physical stores.

POS: point of sale: typically the cash desk where the till, cash drawer and receipt printer are located.

PTV: pendulum test value for degree of slip resistance of floors.

RCP: reflected ceiling plan: a plan of the ceiling drawn from above or overlaid on the floor plan.

RFID: radio-frequency identification.

Store in store: a brand's presence in a department store or other large retailer, often sited on what are known as brand mats.

Shrink or **shrinkage**: reduction in inventory due to shoplifting, employee theft or other errors.

SKU: stock-keeping unit.

Use class: a classification system that recognizes the nature of a building's use. Under the UK's town planning system there are controls in place that limit how a building's use class can be changed.

Vitrine: glass display case.

VM: visual merchandising.

White box: a site which has been prepared as an interior shell only with no fixtures, finishes or equipment.

Anderson, S., and Mesher, L., *Retail Design* (Bloomsbury, 2020)

Bailey, S., and Baker, J., *Visual Merchandising for Fashion* (Bloomsbury, 2020)

Bitgood, S., 'An Analysis of Visitor Circulation: Movement Patterns and the General Value Principle', *Curator: The Museum Journal* (vol. 49, 2010)

British Standards Institute, *BS EN 356:2000 Glass in Building* (BSI, 2000)

British Standards Institute, *BS 4800:2011 Schedule of Paint Colours for Building Purposes* (BSI, 2011)

British Standards Institute, *BS 8300-2:2018 Design of an Accessible and Inclusive Built Environment* (BSI, 2018)

Building Research Establishment, *Loss Prevention Standard LPS 1175, Issue 8.0* (BRE, 2019)

Centre for the Protection of National Infrastructure, *CCTV Within the Workplace* (CPNI, 2020)

Chartered Institution of Building Services Engineers, *Environmental Design* (CIBSE, 2015)

Chartered Institution of Building Services Engineers, *Applications and Activities: HVAC Strategies for Common Building Types* (CIBSE, 2016)

Clarke, R., 'Hot Products: Understanding, Anticipating and Reducing Demand for Stolen Goods', Police Research Series Paper 112 (Home Office, 1999)

Cohen, N., Gattuso, J., and MacLennan-Brown, K., *CCTV Operational Requirements Manual* (Home Office Scientific Development Branch, 2009)

Currie, K., and Nunes, L., *Maximizing Airport Retail Revenue* (InterVISTAS, April 2014)

Davies, R., and Howard, E., 'Issues in Retail Planning Within the United Kingdom', *Built Environment* (14, no. 1, 1988)

Davis, D., *A History of Shopping* (Routledge & Kegan Paul, 1966)

Defoe, D., *The Complete English Tradesman 1726*, 1839 edition (Guttenberg https://www.gutenberg.org/files/14444)

Devine, C., and Flint, R., *Security Glazing: Is It All that It's Cracked Up to Be?* (BRE, 2016)

Dickens, C., *Sketches By Boz 1833–39*, ed. Slater, M. (Phoenix, 1996)

Dudley, R., *Automatic Fire Detection and Alarm Systems* (BRE, 2010)

Evelyn, J., *The Diary of John Evelyn Volume 1, 1620–1664*, ed. Bray, W. (M. Walter Dunne, 1901) (Guttenberg https://www.gutenberg.org/files/41218)

Glass and Glazing Federation, *Safety and Security Glazing Good Practice Guide* (GGF, May 2017)

Health and Safety Executive, *Assessing the Slip Resistance of Flooring* (HSE, May 2012)

Honeycombe, G., *Selfridges: Seventy-Five Years* (Park Lane Press, 1984)

Hughes, C., and Jackson, C., 'Death of the High Street: Identification, Prevention, Reinvention', *Regional Studies, Regional Science* (vol. 2, no. 1, 2015, pp. 237–256)

Imperial College and Kings College London, 'Open/Closed Doors and Air Quality in the Retail Space: Overview of a Study' (Close the Door campaign website, www.closethedoor.org.uk, 2014)

Jukanović, A., *Architectural Lighting Design: A Practical Guide* (The Crowood Press, 2018)

McDonough, W., and Braudgart, M., *Cradle to Cradle: Remaking the Way We Make Things* (Vintage, 2009)

Maitland, B., *Shopping Malls: Planning and Design* (Construction Press, 1985)

Nixon, M., and Aguado, A., *Feature Extraction and Image Processing for Computer Vision*, 4th edn (Academic Press, 2020)

Royal Institute of British Architects, *RIBA Plan of Work 2020 Overview* (RIBA, 2020)

Schneier, M., 'The Chicest Store in Milan Comes to New York' (*The New York Times*, 5 September 2018)

Snoeck, J., and Neerman, P., *The Future of Shopping* (Lannoo Campus, 2017)

Stern, H., 'The Significance of Impulse Buying Today', *Journal of Marketing* (vol. 26, no. 2, April 1962)

Stobart, J., *Spend Spend Spend! A History of Shopping* (The History Press, 2008)

Stow, J., *A Survey of London (Reprinted from the text of 1603, ed. C L Kingsford* (Oxford, 1908) (British History Online http://www.british-history.ac.uk/no-series/survey-of-london-stow/1603)

Summerson, J., *The Classical Language of Architecture* (Thames & Hudson, 1980)

Tilley, N., 'Shoplifting', *Handbook of Crime Science* (Routledge, 2010)

Turner, C., 'Exclusive: Stansted Rises after Major Retail Revamp' (www.trbusiness.com, 9 February 2016)

Underhill, P., *Why We Buy* (Texere, 2000)

Underhill, P., *The Call of the Mall* (Profile Books, 2004)

Walsh, C., 'Shop Design and the Display of Goods in Eighteenth-Century London', *Journal of Design History* (vol. 8, no. 3, 1995, pp. 157–176)

Whitaker, J., *The Department Store* (Thames & Hudson 2011)

Yaeger, L., '10 Corso Como Promises to Radically Reshape the Retail Landscape of New York' (*Vogue*, September 2018)

I T WOULD NOT HAVE BEEN POSSIBLE TO HAVE written this book without the generous help of others. Many freely gave up their time and shared their knowledge and experience and I am indebted to those who provided material for the book, particularly Antonella Azzollini, Stefania Arcari, Jamie Fobert, Max Horwell, Jen Hilton, Daniel Martinho-Corbishley and Benna Schellhorn without whose help I could not have included the case studies.

My thanks also go to Melda Bur, Martin Campbell Davies, Alan Cheyne, Alastair Craven, Lucy Dewick-Tew, Jeremy Grove, Bart Higgins, Maida Hot, Barry Maitland, Roger Miles, Anne Pitcher, P.J. Ward and Ian Warwick.

Lastly, thank you to my wife Gillian, who tolerated my addiction to store visiting and mall exploration.

PICTURE CREDITS

All photographs, drawings and images are by the author unless stated otherwise.

Photos by Sue Barr appear with kind permission of Jamie Fobert Architects.

Photos by Olivier Hess appear with kind permission of Jamie Fobert Architects.

Photo by Andrew Meredith appears with kind permission of Selfridges & Co.

Photo by Stefan Reimschuessel appears with kind permission of Portview Fit-Out Ltd.